Make Your Business

Take A Strategic Approach

■ SMART STRATEGIES SERIES ■

Make Your Business Grow

Take A Strategic Approach

David Irwin

INTERNATIONAL THOMSON BUSINESS PRESS
I(T)P® An International Thomson Publishing Company

London ● Bonn ● Boston ● Johannesburg ● Madrid ● Melbourne ● Mexico City ● New York ● Paris
Singapore ● Tokyo ● Toronto ● Albany, NY ● Belmont, CA ● Cincinnati, OH ● Detroit, MI

Make Your Business Grow

Copyright © 1998 David Irwin

First published by International Thomson Business Press

 A division of International Thomson Publishing Inc.
The ITP logo is a trademark under licence

British Library Cataloguing-in-Publication Data
A catalogue record for this book is available from the British Library

First edition 1998

Typeset by LaserScript Limited, Mitcham, Surrey
Printed in the UK by TJ International, Padstow, Cornwall

ISBN 1–86152–204–5

International Thomson Business Press
Berkshire House
168–173 High Holborn
London WC1V 7AA
UK

http://www.itbp.com

Contents

Preface   vi
Acknowledgements   vii

CHAPTER ONE
The importance of strategic thinking   1

CHAPTER TWO
Looking out   19

CHAPTER THREE
Looking ahead   48

CHAPTER FOUR
Looking inwards   66

CHAPTER FIVE
Defining a direction   84

CHAPTER SIX
Defining objectives and measuring performance   105

CHAPTER SEVEN
Managing for success   134

CHAPTER EIGHT
Strategy checklist to help your business grow   163

References   167
Index   169

Preface

I was travelling recently and came across this description of contentment from an ancient Roman poet:

> The qualities that make for a happy and genial life, are these: a small estate with fruitful vineyards, a fire to curtail the rigours of winter, a contented mind, a strong and healthy body, frankness tempered by tact, congenial associates, happy guests, a table spread with simple meats, wine not in excess but enough to drive away care, yet virtuous with all, sound sleep to make dark hours fly, no longing for change, just contentment with what you are, no fear of death, nor yet a desire for it.

But for some people, especially people who are running a business, that may not be enough. You will be ambitious to achieve rather more – to make your business grow bigger or, perhaps, just to grow better and to reap the rewards. Even Deng Xiao Ping said that 'to get rich is glorious'. To do that, you need a strategic framework – to offer guidance as you consider and make decisions in relation to your business, rather than being a straightjacket – which will help you plan your business's future development. You probably already develop strategies for many of the things that you do. If you're going into an important negotiating session, for example, you will think in advance about what you want to achieve, how you hope to get it, what you are prepared to offer, and the scope for compromise. This book aims to look at the wider picture of business strategy – to discover where you are now, to decide where you want to go, and to determine how you can get there. Research by Barclays Bank suggests that 60 per cent of small businesses plan no more than one month ahead. Achieving success will require a longer time horizon, but developing an effective framework does not have to be overly time consuming – and the time that is spent will be well rewarded.

This book is for owner managers of businesses employing, say, up to 50 people and for managers in larger businesses with responsibility for an autonomous division or department. It is intended to help you look at your business from a strategic perspective – defining your purpose, reviewing the environment, considering what drives you and your business and setting goals – and then regularly assessing your performance. Small businesses have sometimes been defined not by size but as businesses which are 'doing things for the first time'. This book will be of particular interest to those people who are just beginning to think about strategy and long-term planning, who are confused by the different definitions that abound and who simply want to apply some simple ideas to help to develop their business.

In an effort to relate the theory to everyday practicalities, I have drawn examples and case studies from both small and large businesses and the occasional non-profit organization, as well as including practical suggestions to help you put theory into practice in your own business.

Entrepreneurs are sometimes regarded as risk takers. I see entrepreneurs as people who take calculated risks, who take steps to mitigate risks. Having a strategic framework is one way of ensuring that risk is reduced; indeed, the evidence suggests that businesses which have strategies for growth are far more likely to succeed.

Being in business is challenging. It is frustrating. It can be rewarding. Above all it should be fun. Having a strategy will, I hope, enable you to reduce the frustration and increase the fun and the reward. Good Luck!

David Irwin

Acknowledgements

This book has come about from a desire to summarize at least some of what I have learned from working over many years with a wide range of businesses and not for profit organizations both in the UK and internationally.

I am very grateful to my clients and to the other businesses both small and large who have inspired the examples and case studies. Particular thanks are due to: Andrews Plastics; Flexible Learning Associates; Fulprint; Giveway Internet; John Lewis Partnership; Hydro Technologies; Octo Industrial Design; PI Engineering; Solution Design Consultants; Xtralite; Yeoman Pressings. Thank you also to all those who have allowed me to quote from their own published materials in order to illustrate the points that I am trying to make.

I would particularly like to thank Alan Bretherton, Sandy Ogilvie, Julie Lewthwaite and Julian Thomas for reading drafts, for their helpful comments and for their encouragement and to Kim Allen for her skilful editing. Thank you to Julia Watson and Pat Heywood for their assistance and unfailing humour in typing and correcting innumerable drafts.

Very importantly, let me say a big thank you to my wife, Jane, for her love and patience throughout the time that I have been writing this book.

CHAPTER ONE

The importance of strategic thinking

The strategy of the gardener

Do you garden? If so, you've probably had experience of going to your nearest garden centre, buying some colourful plants that take your fancy and then planting them in what seems like an appropriate place. Then spring comes and you realize that one flowerbed has no spring bulbs. You may have decided on a whim that a few plants in pots would look nice on the patio. Or else you're so involved in getting one flowerbed to look right that you fail to consider how it fits in with the rest of the garden. Periodically you stand at the bedroom window and survey the garden as a whole – looking at how the plants in each bed complement each other, how all the flowerbeds work together, how the trees and the plants in tubs provide a backdrop. And you think about how the plants are developing, how big the bushes will become, how the gaps can be filled and how long it will take before any new plants reach their potential. You might also look at the adjoining gardens. Do you need to complement plants there? Do they provide competition – a hedge of lalandia, for example, will drain all the water and nutrients out of the soil so you need to take appropriate action. And you'll certainly have weeds with which to contend. I never fail to be amazed how easily they take root and how quickly they spread.

As you continue to garden, you'll undoubtedly learn and modify what you do as a result. You'll discover, for example, that frost kills your bedding plants and hanging baskets – so you keep those plants inside until the last of the frosts have gone. If you have family, you'll probably pass on that learning. You might do background research – to discover how to have flowerbeds flowering for most of the year, or to find plants which will grow in that corner of the garden which never sees the sun, or to determine whether your plants prefer acidic or alkaline soil. If you are worried about the likely rainfall you may choose plants which are happy with little water. Or you may install a waterbutt and collect all the rainfall that you can for use in the garden.

Do you look for ideas in others people's gardens, or at public gardens, or at garden centres? Do you ever think about why you garden? Is it to provide a safe environment for the children or a relaxing place for you to sit? Do you ever think about major changes, like building a greenhouse or sinking a fish pond?

If you are a particularly keen gardener, you probably have a timetable of things to do – planting, weeding, feeding – over the year. There will be occasions when you take preventative action, such as putting weedkiller on your paths or weed and feed on the lawn in spring. You will sometimes need to take corrective action – pulling up weeds, or using spot weedkiller. There will be some things you do regularly – like mowing the lawn. Some things you might only do occasionally, but might require longer term planning and may have implications. A tree for example, may take a long time to grow to its potential. A rhododendron requires acidic soil, so you cannot grow your irises next to it.

Do all of these activities ring bells? If so, you have a purpose (maintaining a tidy garden in which you can relax and the children can play), goals (building the fish pond), an overview of strengths and weaknesses (gazing down from the bedroom window) and of opportunities and threats (new ideas, rampaging dandelions and late spring frost), a vision (what the garden will look like in six or twelve months), a strategy (how everything fits together) and an operational plan (a timetable and specified activities). A strategy for your business is not so different.

You will find your gardening easier if you match the right resources to the required tasks. For example, you can aerate the lawn with a fork, but it's easier with one of those revolving spikers. Without either, the task is impossible. Using the right fertilizer at the right time in the right quantity is important – otherwise you might kill your plants. Once again, business is not so different.

The strategy of the football manager

If you don't have a garden, or don't like gardening, perhaps you prefer football. Imagine, for a moment, that you are the manager of a premier league football club. The, somewhat ambitious, goal that you have set for yourself and the club is winning the European Champions' Cup.

You have a vision of your club at the pinnacle of European football – and your goal is the embodiment of that vision – but you recognize that it may take some time to get there. So you set milestones. This year, you aim to finish in the top four of the league – to give you experience in the UEFA cup. Next year, you aim to win the league championship. And the year after that, the Champions' Cup.

Your over-arching goal is quite clear. Your purpose is clear – to build a team capable of winning at the highest levels. For each match, the mission will be clear – to win, or maybe it won't be quite so clear – you may need extra goals, for example, to improve your goal difference.

As the manager, you will be worried about weaknesses and threats. Weaknesses, perhaps, are those poor defenders or lack of money to buy new players or insufficient players of appropriate quality to cope with the inevitable injuries. Threats come from other clubs who might tempt away your star players. But you will also note your strengths (and build on them) and look for opportunities (buying star players, nurturing home grown talent, selling satellite TV rights, etc.).

You may decide that your goals can best be realized simply by buying players – or you may take a longer term view, by aiming to identify, recruit and develop younger players. They will probably be more loyal and more committed – and if you should decide to sell, give a better return. Most likely you will recognize a need to strike a balance between these two to fit the circumstances. You will need the courage to sell players who, despite expectations, do not fit the team.

You will endeavour to build the squad into a team – so that all the players know what to expect of all the rest and so that everyone can rely on and trust everyone else, even when things are going badly.

You will engage in regular intelligence gathering – not only to look for the opportunities mentioned above, but also to understand how your opposing teams play. For each match, you will then attempt to match your resources (strikers, defenders, midfield) to your best assessment of the requirement. This will result in different players and different formations for different matches. This individual approach to each game is tactics. Having picked the team for a particular match, there'll be a pre-match briefing, in which the specific approach to the game will be planned and rehearsed, in which contingency plans will be discussed, etc.

After each game, you'll do a debrief with the team. What went right? What went wrong? How can you improve next time? What weaknesses were identified? How can they be overcome? What were the strengths? How can they be built on? What specific training might be required?

The strategy of the chess player

The goal in a single game of chess is clear; for world class players, the goal may be to win the world title, but that requires many little steps – and each step is winning a game.

Unlike the business world, of course, every game of chess starts from the same position and both players are equal – well, more or less equal. In some ways, the starting position is the most difficult position. How do you decide what to do first. Once you've made a move, you cannot go back and start again.

Each move you make needs to achieve two things – it needs to help to build a defence against your opponent, or at least not leave a chink through which you can be attacked, and it needs to advance your own cause. You need to think ahead, therefore. You need to think about the moves you would like to make – that is you need a plan – individual moves are insignificant, but together they become a strategy. Second, you need to think about the moves your opponent might make – that is, you need foresight.

World class companies

Many people these days talk about 'world class' companies. But what is a world class company? And do you want to be one? You don't have to be world class to grow, of course. But if you do have the aspiration and potential to grow you may well be interested in what characterizes successful companies – and you may choose to strive to emulate some or all of those characteristics. Some people may believe such characteristics are only relevant to larger businesses, but they will become increasingly important to smaller businesses: as larger firms continue to shed labour, to sub-contract more, and to develop stronger relationships with their suppliers, they will increasingly expect their suppliers to follow their lead at least in terms of innovation and quality and values.

Research undertaken in 1994 by the DTI amongst some of the best UK companies suggest that winning companies:

- are led by visionary, enthusiastic champions of change;

- unlock the potential of all of their staff;

- know their customers;

- constantly introduce new, differentiated products and services;

- exceed their customers' expectations (DTI/CBI, 1994).

More recently, the RSA has looked at the success factors that they believe will characterize 'Tomorrow's Company' (RSA, 1995). In particular, they think Tomorrow's Company will:

- clearly define and communicate its purpose and values;

- develop a framework for performance measurement which is based on its purpose and values and the relationship between them;

- value reciprocal relationships with stakeholders recognizing that this will ultimately improve returns for shareholders;

- actively work to develop and maintain positive relationships with stakeholders;

- expect to act in ways which maintain its licence to operate and its reputation.

Richard Onians, managing partner at Baring Venture Partners Ltd, asserts (Onians, 1995) that world class businesses:

- are owned and managed by people who are experienced in and capable of exploiting international opportunities;

- have designed their products or services to be attractive globally in terms of price, quality and availability;

- are managed to sustain their competitive advantage in order to be consistently profitable.

Clem Sunter, head of scenario planning at Anglo American Corporation, believes (Sunter, 1992) winning companies:

- maximize the advantages to be gained from rapidly developing information and communication technologies, not just as part of their process of horizon scanning – but in order to hear the important news first;

- regard personal development, training and education of their staff as a *sine qua non* for success since, generally, it is people who give businesses their unique strengths;

- maintain small head offices, delegating and empowering as much as possible, motivating staff through maximizing autonomy, but holding them accountable as well, within a framework provided by a clear sense of purpose and a set of core values;

- encourage technological innovation, understanding that often this is a random process, rather than always happening to order;

- look at what the customer needs and can afford and then work backwards to provide a product or service that meets the need within the given price as, for example, Canon did with their desktop copier;

- stress ethics and values, recognizing that increasingly customers are concerned about the environment and about certain developing world labour practices, for example;

- though not everyone will agree with this, pioneer new markets in developing countries – because this is where, as their populations continue to expand rapidly, the bulk of potential customers will live.

I would echo all these characteristics, and would add a couple more exhibited by businesses aiming to grow:

- acute awareness of the environment which they constantly and actively scan;

- a propensity to develop via strategic alliances and joint ventures.

Achieving all this is clearly an extremely tall order, But, as many new and growing businesses demonstrate, it is not impossible. Is it worth it? Yes – it is! Kleinwort Benson believe strongly that companies which espouse the Tomorrow's Company principles actually perform better than other companies, actually increasing shareholder value more than companies that simply say that their objective is to increase shareholder value. They have even launched a unit trust which invests in companies they believe adopt the inclusive approach and, so far at least, it has outperformed the FT-SE100. The starting point has to be a suitable strategic framework. How to develop one is what the rest of this book is all about.

To be successful, the most important requirement is to identify a market for your product or service and then to exploit it. Successful exploitation requires you to develop and implement a realistic strategy. Furthermore, you will need to communicate that strategy to staff – to motive them – and to funders – to gain and retain their support. You may need to manage innovation – ensuring that process or product developments are delivered on time and to budget. Indeed, Peter Drucker

(1968) suggests that the two key basic functions of any business are simply marketing and innovation. You will need to monitor what is happening, through an effective management information system, in order to exercise control. Last, but by no means least, you will need to recruit and develop and motivate staff with the competence and experience to help you achieve success.

Strategic thinking in business

The overall concept of strategy in gardening or football or chess is very simple. You have a goal and you do what is necessary to achieve that goal. In business, the concept is just as simple, though achieving a successful outcome may require more effort than the gardening. There are, of course, expectations and pressures on business both from within and outside the organization.

All businesses have three important groups of stakeholders – all with their own expectations – the owners, the customers and the staff, though there may be other stakeholders such as suppliers or the wider community.

Customers will be looking for a product or service which fulfils their needs and which represents good value for money. They will only pay a premium price for a premium product and even then only if they can see the benefits. Unless your product is always a one-off sale, you will be keen to develop a continuing relationship with your customers. Retaining existing customers is considerably cheaper and easier than finding new customers, but it does require effort. Customers might be concerned about your long-term survival and prosperity because they rely on you to provide a much needed product or service. Customers will, therefore, have expectations of your business.

The owners will have expectations. If you are the sole owner, you will already know what you expect of the business. If there is more than one owner, particularly if the other shareholders do not work in the business, they will be looking for a return on the capital they have invested in the business. This may be yours (and your partners') but you should still be aiming for a return better than you would achieve if the money was, say, in the building society. If you have external investors, they will be looking for capital appreciation and evidence that their investment is being well managed. This suggests a need for financial objectives, not necessarily intended to maximize the possible return, but at least set to provide a reasonable return. Remember, too, that money will be needed for reinvestment and growth.

Staff, too, will have expectations. They will be looking for realistic rewards for their efforts on behalf of the business allied with career and development opportunities and an environment in which they are happy to work.

Bob Garratt, commenting on the Institute of Directors' publication, 'Standards for the Board' (Garratt, 1966), describes a number of potential conflicts – what he calls directoral dilemmas. These dilemmas apply to anyone who is running a business:

- The proprietor must endeavour to be entrepreneurial and to drive the business forward whilst at the same time retaining effective control.

- The proprietor must be sufficiently knowledgeable about all the activities of the business to be answerable for its actions (easy when small, but increasingly difficult as the business grows), yet must be able to stand back from day to day activities in order to take a longer term view of where the business is going and how to get there.

- The proprietor must be aware of short term and local issues whilst also keeping up to date with the trends in the competitive market place and in the wider environment.

- The proprietor needs to focus on the commercial needs of the business whilst acting responsibly and fairly to staff, business pressures and, particularly as the business grows, to the wider community.

Ideally your strategic thinking will include consideration of how you meet the expectations of your different stakeholders and of how you address the possible dilemmas.

It seems that a great number of books about strategy, or some element of it, are written every year. Some of them have a simple message, though in practice it is not always easy to see how to apply that message in a smaller business. Others are more complex, and the message itself is less clear, let alone how to apply it.

This, I hope, will be a simple book, with a simple message. The simple message is that strategy gets you 'from here to there'. If you take control of the strategy, you can achieve great goals. And the strategy itself can be simple – indeed, the simpler the strategy, the easier it will be to implement, and the easier also it will be to inspire the business's staff to put the strategy into practice.

What, then, are the characteristics of a successful strategy?

I think they are these:

- First, businesses must know their purpose – their mission, if you prefer – which defines what the business does and, probably, the values it holds dear;

- Second, businesses need to know where they want to go. They must have vision – an idea of their desired future state. This is linked to ambition – demonstrated by using what American academics, James Collins and Gerry Porras (1994) refer to as 'big hairy audacious goals'.

- Lastly, they need at least some idea of where the rest of the world is going – that is, foresight.

To maximize your chances of success in business, you simply need to apply the ideas outlined for the gardener, the football manager and the chess player. You need a purpose, you need goals, you need a plan, you need to monitor your performance against the plan and you may need occasionally to take corrective action to stay on course. A clear and simple direction will make leading the business far easier. To be effective you need regularly to look at your business's strengths and weaknesses and at the opportunities and threats posed by the environment in which you operate.

If you look up the word 'strategy' in the dictionary you'll see that it originally applied to the conduct of war. The *Oxford English Dictionary*, for example, defines strategy first of all as 'the planning and directing of the whole operation of a campaign of war' and only second as 'a plan or policy of this kind or to achieve something'. In war, the goal is clear – to win. Your strategy sets out how you plan to do this. As with football, individual battles are covered by 'tactics'.

Strategy defines what you do to get you from where you are now to where you want to be, say, in three or five years' time. Businesses set a purpose and define goals. The strategy must support the purpose, it must fit the environment in which the business works but will be constrained by resource availability. It must be action focused. In Drucker's (1968) words, strategy 'converts what you want to do into accomplishment'.

Many small businesses think of strategic or long-term planning as something that is only undertaken by large businesses. Henry Mintzberg (1994) argues that strategic planning is a contradiction in terms in that it is not possible to plan and to be strategic simultaneously. Andy Grove, CEO of Intel, points out (Grove, 1997) that strategic plans deal with events far in the future – sometimes so far in the future that they are of little relevance to what you do today. On the other hand, strategic actions take place in the present. Those actions do, of course, need to be consistent with longer term plans. Grove goes on to suggest that having committed yourself to a particular direction, you should go for it as fast as possible. Strategic thinking is simply a way of thinking about how to position your business *vis-à-vis* your customers and your competitors. Many businesses do have a clear idea of where they are heading and how they expect to get there; many more appear simply to be 'in business' without really having any clear vision. Stop for a moment . . . can you imagine the future? Of course you can – you have hopes and aspirations and you may already have goals and targets. So you have what Gary Hamel and C.K. Prahalad (1994) call 'strategic intent' – a desire to shape your future and an idea of what that future might look like. They go on to suggest that a strategic intent provides a framework of three elements: a sense of direction, a sense of discovery and a sense of destiny.

The businesses that survive and prosper are those that meet their customers' needs by providing benefits to them at prices which cover the cost of providing them and provide both sufficient profit for reinvestment and also a share of the profit or a dividend which satisfies the owners or the shareholders. To do this effectively, it is important to think strategically but it is also important to plan if the strategy is to be implemented effectively. Do you know how you intend to achieve your aspirations? If so, you have a strategy. It doesn't have to be complicated; indeed, the simpler you keep it, the easier it is to remember. Taking a strategic view of your business will help you to think about your over-arching goals and how you expect to achieve them. Having a strategy should not be seen as a straightjacket – but as a framework enabling you both to keep the business on course but also to exploit appropriate opportunities as they arise. The Japanese call this *hoshin kanri* – direction management. The strategy must be flexible, but without some long-term objectives you will not be able to manage your direction.

Drucker (1968) notes that businesses need to focus on the external environment in order to create a customer. Similarly, Michael Porter (1985) argues that the way a business positions itself in the market place is of paramount importance. Having found your customers you then need to satisfy their needs. The two most important functions for any business then, are generating orders and fulfilling those orders.

Gerry Johnson and Kevan Scholes (1993) note that effective strategies:

- match the business's activities to the environment;

- match the business's activities to its available resources or its ability to attract extra resources;

- reflect the values and expectations of the business's stakeholders, particularly, their owners;

- impact on a business's long-term direction.

More specifically, your task is to match effectively the business's competences (that is, its knowledge, expertise and experience) and resources with the opportunities and threats created by the market place. Indeed, Gary Hamel (1997) argues that you should not define your business by what you sell but by identifying your fundamental capabilities.

Thinking strategically is important for every business, but it is particularly important for the smaller business, since smaller businesses may be more vulnerable than larger businesses to changes in the market place. Every business has a strategy of some sort, even if it is never articulated. However, an emergent strategy, i.e. one that emerges as the business progresses, is unlikely to be as successful as a strategy which is planned in advance, i.e. one where the business is being proactive rather than reactive and where the business is creating opportunities rather than responding to them.

If you are reading this book, the chances are that you want to develop a strategy which will help you to grow. As you grow, however, you should expect to have to adjust your strategy. It may be worth mentioning, therefore, the likely stages of growth in your business and the ways in which businesses grow.

Stages of growth

American academic, Larry Greiner (1972) has suggested that businesses grow – or fail – through combinations of evolution and revolution – progressing through stages of creativity, direction, delegation, co-ordination and collaboration. I have observed similar phases amongst businesses with which I have worked.

During start-up, founders concentrate on creating a product or service, identifying potential customers and developing a market. They have probably started because they have spotted an opportunity, but they often lack management and commercial experience. This may be worse where a business is started by a technologist whose motivation stems from solving an interesting technical problem rather than from a desire to found a viable business.

In the early stages, the proprietor is seen as the leader. There is little or no structure. If there are staff, there is probably a club culture. Communication is informal. Initial growth may be rapid, with conse-

FIGURE 1.1 Stages of growth

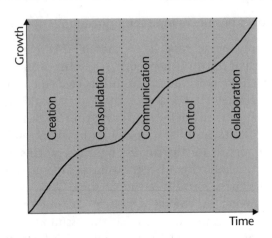

quent problems of cash flow management. Control is limited to simple bookkeeping and managing within cash limits. Resources are limited at this initial stage.

As the business becomes established in the market place, it consolidates. Typically, the proprietor becomes more comfortable with the control aspects, is able to set more realistic targets, based on history rather than solely on forecasts, and begins to put in place reporting procedures, to keep lenders happy for example. This frees up time to concentrate on marketing. If the business can do this successfully, then it will start to grow.

As the number of staff grows, communication becomes more important. Effective financial control calls for greater proceduralization. The proprietor may become more of a manager – or else recruits someone as manager. Management focuses on efficiency. The organizational structure is probably hierarchical, focusing on role. Work is delegated, but the role culture requires close control, which can only be achieved through more communications becoming more formal. The business may be divided into cost centres, with managers held accountable for financial performance without necessarily being given full responsibility.

The centre imposes greater control to ensure profitability. This can lead to bureaucracy and procedures taking precedence over problem solving. The hierarchy becomes restrictive with the likelihood of conflict between following procedures and taking initiative and the consequent demotivation of staff. Continuing growth, however, requires that proprietors 'let go' – to trust others to act in the best interests of the business.

This leads to better delegation, giving staff greater freedom to act on their own initiative. There is more emphasis on teamworking, with a focus on task and problem solving, and collaboration. The hierarchy evolves into a matrix type management structure, with greater mutual trust and confidence. The business is now likely to be divided into profit centres. There is less emphasis on rigid procedures and more emphasis on mutual goal setting. Control is exercised through regular management meetings, possibly allied with centralized or joint control over investment proposals.

If you have grown a business to the stage where it employs a number of people engaged in a range of activities, you will probably have experienced these stages.

These stages of growth are mentioned here because the points at which a business recognizes a need to move on – changing management structures, changing control systems, etc. – often coincide with a need for a rethink about strategy and, sometimes, a need for more investment. Furthermore external financiers will have matching requirements – strong management, effective control systems, etc. Businesses which understand where they are on the growth curve will be in a better position to argue their case with prospective funders.

Become a learning organization

W. Edwards Deming, one of the originators of total quality management, conceived the idea of continuous improvement, embodied in the cycle of Plan-Do-Check-Act. (See Vonderembse and White, 1996.)

First, set out a plan for what you want to do. Then do it. Check carefully what you have done. Is there scope for improvement? If so, take appropriate action. Amend your plan accordingly. Just like the football manager!

As you plan, whether at strategic level or operational level, you will find that there are four key steps as shown in Figure 1.2. First, you need to do some analysis – of the environment, of the market place, of other organizations in the same field, etc. Then you are in a position to make a choice. The next step is to implement that choice. Lastly you will need to review progress and exercise control. Ideally, as the business progresses, you will all be learning. There is a need to capture the results of that learning so that the whole business can benefit.

FIGURE 1.2   The Deming wheel

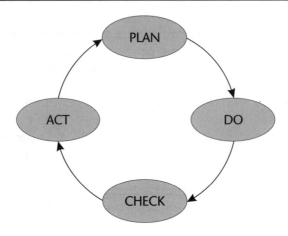

Exploring strategy

There are many external pressures on any organization. These include competitors' activities, requirements of both customers and suppliers, legislation, inflation, rapidly changing technology, staff needs, spotting opportunities, recognizing threats, etc. You have little or no control over the environment in which you operate. But you can watch carefully and respond to the signals. Ideally, you will want to take an overview of what might happen to the external factors and make a stab at defining the environment in which your organization will operate in the future.

One of the problems, at least for me, in writing a book about strategy and growth is in trying to determine a logical order for the book that covers everything and that avoids repetition. I have concluded that it is almost impossible. If you already have an understanding of the key requirements for strategic thinking, then you may simply like to hop around. If you have little idea, I suggest that you start by reading the summary and checklist in the last chapter. This will give you a feel for how everything fits together. Whilst I have tried hard to avoid repetition, inevitably some topics are introduced at one point in the book and then covered in more detail later.

Chapter Two explains the importance of looking out from the business, scanning the environment and gathering marketing intelligence. It also touches on the topic of benchmarking – comparing your performance with others to identify ways in which you could do things better. Chapter Three extends this to scanning the horizon and looking ahead. Forecasting is difficult, if not impossible, but a degree of foresight will be valuable.

In Chapter Four, attention turns to the business itself, looking at values and culture, at strengths and weaknesses. There are just as many internal constraints imposed on business. How much money can be raised? Does the board of directors have the appropriate skills? Are skilled staff available? What are the aspirations and ambitions of the board and staff? These factors will all constrain the business's activities and growth.

The board and senior staff of any organization have to cut through all this, defining a purpose and goals, keeping track so that you can run your business with the resources available and ensure that the external pressures are managed in such a way that they do not overwhelm you. Chapter Five covers the concepts of purpose, goals and vision. Chapter Six builds on that, describing how the business's strategic objectives help towards achieving the goals and how they can be broken down into everyday operational objectives.

Chapter Seven explains the importance of leadership and organizational structure in order to manage effectively your most important resource, your staff.

This probably all sounds very daunting, but it is easy to break down the planning process into a number of levels. Henry Mintzberg (1994) argues that planning is about preparing for the inevitable, pre-empting the undesirable and controlling the controllable. Without at least some planning to determine how you will achieve your goals, there will be nothing to control.

There is no magic formula for success. Management writers and academics like to coin new terms like total quality management or Kaizen or business process re-engineering. But simply introducing these ideas does little to help the business. What does help the business is having a clear idea of what your customers or potential customers want; a clear idea of how you can deliver your product or service to them at a cost lower than the price they are prepared to pay; and, a clear idea of how to stay ahead of your competitors.

Planning can help with:

- *Focusing ideas* – the process of planning forces you and your staff to think through and refine their organizations, goals and objectives.

- *Assessing viability* – regularly ensuring that there will be sufficient income to cover all the costs and make a profit.

- *Maintaining control* – the most effective weapon for control is knowledge – knowing where the business is now, how it is performing and where it is going.

- *Developing foresight* – planning as a continuous activity encourages the identification of opportunities; a plan can then be formulated to take advantage of these. In addition, planning helps in the identification of threats, so that these can be avoided or mitigated.

Bob Garratt (1996) suggests that there is a simple three level hierarchy, which the Chinese and Greeks have used for thousands of years – policy, strategy and operations.

Policy sets a long-term view and reflects how the organization sees itself within the external environment. Strategic thinking is similarly long term, but is more about the internal operation of the organization; operations are clearly internal and tend to be short term. The way that the organization operates will affect the way it is perceived by outsiders and the way in which the business may find itself accountable if it 'misbehaves'.

Look, listen and learn

Some people argue that a strategy is not really necessary and point to examples of businesses that have succeeded, apparently, without a strategy. Whilst it is true that many entrepreneurs do not ever write down their strategy in any formal sense, most successful entrepreneurs do have a clear idea of where they are going and how they are going to get there. Research by Baring Venture Partners amongst businesses in which they have invested (Onians, 1995) suggests that spending time to develop a strategy is worthwhile: 'In our experience, developing an appropriate strategy for a business is usually accomplished. Failure is only rarely caused by a misguided strategy.'

Defining a purpose and agreeing goals which reflect your values and beliefs will provide you with the framework that you need. Creating a strategy will put in place the long-term guidance to enable the business to move towards achievement of its goals and consequent success.

Redefining those long-term objectives as short-term operational targets will provide suitable milestones. Measuring performance will enable you to see how well the business is doing and, if necessary, take corrective action.

Do not forget to watch the market place and the wider environment. Changes may affect your policy and will almost certainly affect your strategic objectives.

FIGURE 1.3

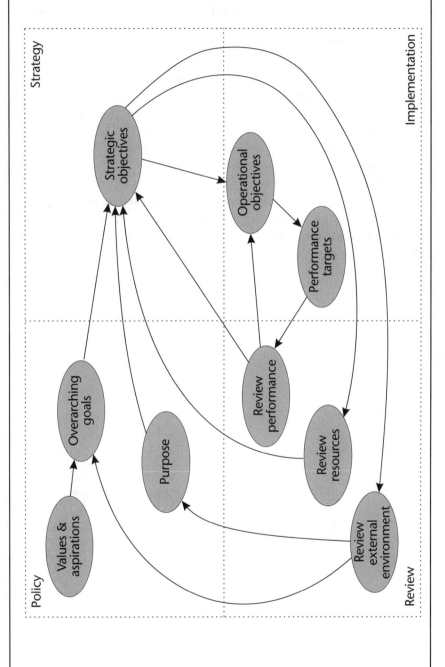

As you start to achieve your goals, set new ones. Even in a small company a three or five year strategy will probably be in need of renewal half way through the time period. Failure to redefine goals regularly probably indicates that effective review of performance, resources, resource availability and the environment is not being undertaken and the business is drifting rather than being driven along. Aim to maximize use of your resources, but do not over extend yourself.

Remember that the ideal strategy is simple, clear and measurable – and will help you to ensure that you achieve your stake in the future.

Tom Peters, who co-wrote *In Search of Excellence* has since suggested 'excellent firms don't believe in excellence – only in constant improvement and constant change.'

Above all – aim to enjoy yourself. Running a business is a challenge. It demands 110 per cent effort. And not knowing where you are going will be extremely frustrating. But it can also be immensely exciting and rewarding and fun – and made all the easier if you have a strategic framework as guidance.

CHAPTER TWO

Looking out

External influences on your business

There are many factors both inside and outside your business which will affect your ability to achieve your goals and which will therefore influence the strategy you choose to adopt. In this chapter we will look at Porter's five forces model, at assessing what is happening in the environment, at customer profiling and at spotting best practice. The chapter will conclude by identifying areas of opportunity and areas of weakness. The next chapter will take this further by looking ahead.

The market place

Five forces

Professor Michael Porter, of the Harvard Business School, has developed what he calls the five forces model (Porter, 1980) to explain the key competitive forces which impinge on any business. The forces are inter-firm rivalry, the threat of new entrants, the threat of substitute products, the bargaining power of suppliers and the bargaining power of customers. Some people now add a sixth force: the power of complementors – businesses without which your own product or service would be irrelevant but which are necessary because buyers see the products as being complementary. Software writers need people to buy computers; hi-fi manufacturers need records and CDs; car manufacturers need fuel companies.

It doesn't require much inspiration to realize that competitors may cause you problems if you are aiming to sell exactly the same product or service to exactly the same target market. If you find yourself in this

FIGURE 2.1   External forces

Source: Adapted from the Five Forces Model, (Porter, 1980)

position then you will need to do something about perhaps reducing price (often difficult for a small business), or improving the service you offer, or moving into a different market.

Focus

Intel, for example, had built itself and its reputation as a developer and manufacturer of computer memory. But the increasing competition from cost reducing and quality improving Japanese competitors led Intel out of the memory business and encouraged it to concentrate on microprocessors.

My father-in-law used to have a grocery shop, but the advent of supermarkets offered the same products at a much lower price. As a result, he closed the grocery and started a newsagency. Some small groceries, have recently been hitting back, by opening at hours that are more convenient for shoppers, or by offering more specialist provisions. In other words, they are competing on service.

When I was young, garages sold petrol and supermarkets didn't exist. Supermarkets sprang up to offer a lower cost way of shopping and saw an opportunity to sell low cost petrol as a further way of attracting customers. Petrol stations have now begun to hit back – increasingly offering a wide range of grocery provisions. Shell Select, for example, is now one of the country's largest retailers of sandwiches.

There is always the possibility of new entrants, particularly where the barriers to entry are relatively low. Unless you have invented a new product or developed some proprietary software, say, you will always be vulnerable to new entrants. And even if you do have something totally different, if it is successful, bigger and more powerful firms will quickly come into, and probably dominate, the market place. Once again, your best strategy, probably, is to offer something different to customers.

The threat of substitute products should not be overlooked. Look what happened to IBM when the personal computer took off. Even though the IBM design became the *de facto* standard, IBM never quite believed personal computers would take such a large part of the computer market. Look at the Swiss watch industry – tied to the manufacture of mechanical watches – and nearly destroyed by cheaper and more accurate electronic watches from Japan. Or the manufacturers of slide rules who were destroyed by the advent of the electronic calculator. Remember that people do not buy products – they buy benefits. That is, they are buying something which will enable them to achieve whatever it is they want to achieve – a lawn mower provides the benefit of short grass, a car provides the benefit of transport – or maybe acts as a status symbol!

Suppliers have tremendous bargaining power, especially if your business is small and they are large and more so still if you have little choice about where to go for your supplies. Procter and Gamble, for example, make specific demands of the supermarkets who stock their products in terms of the amount of shelf space and prominence they get – and they have staff who go round and check. The more competition that there is in a market place, then the more the power of suppliers will be reduced. You may, nevertheless, still be vulnerable in terms of delivery timescales, quality and price. There may be a high cost, or it may be next to impossible to switch to an alternative supplier. If you build computers, you may be totally reliant on Intel microprocessors and Microsoft operating systems.

Customers also have bargaining power. Ultimately, they can take their custom elsewhere. They will make demands of you in the same way that you do of your suppliers – specification and quality, price, delivery timescales, etc. if you are a sub-contractor, your customers will be particularly demanding if what you are supplying represents a high proportion of the selling price of their product.

Some companies have spotted this. Sony, for example, bought Columbia studios and set up their own music label to sell 'content' to buyers of their hardware. As they discovered, however, the skills in developing and marketing new electronic products are rather different to the skills necessary to develop and market talent.

Customer profiling

You need to profile your ideal customers accurately. The more precisely you can describe them, the easier it will be not only to offer a product or service that meets their specified needs but also to target them more carefully with your promotional activities. This is particularly necessary for small businesses. With limited resources you cannot hope to compete in all available markets. For a small business this either means finding a highly specialized 'niche' in a national or international market, or tailoring a product or service to compete in local markets. One way of developing profiles is through market segmentation.

The Burton Group originally manufactured and sold men's suits through a chain of stores. But in the early 1980s, they started to think carefully about the market and began to segment it – by age of purchaser style, cost, etc. – and concentrated on offering well designed, value for money clothes which they marketed carefully. Indeed this was so successful that they came to see their own strengths as design and marketing and eventually stopped manufacturing themselves in favour of sub-contracting it all.

The way they have segmented the market for women's clothes is shown in Figure 2.2 (Burton Group, 1993). Apart from Debenhams, a department store which Burton took over, all their shops are focused at a specific, single gender market. Debenhams, as a department store, always had a wider target market which it retained even as part of the Burton Group. Burton belatedly recognized the lack of fit and decided to demerge Debenhams.

Superdrug, the fast growing pharmacy, has segmented the market for cosmetics by looking at Kylies, Sharons and plain Janes! Microsoft, in segmenting the business market, has identified start ups, steady state, dynamic growers and vulnerables.

You, too, can segment the market. Of course you do not have to sell to more than one segment – at least not at the start. But segmenting the market can help you to define your target market more accurately.

FIGURE 2.2   Burton Group Segmentation: Womenswear

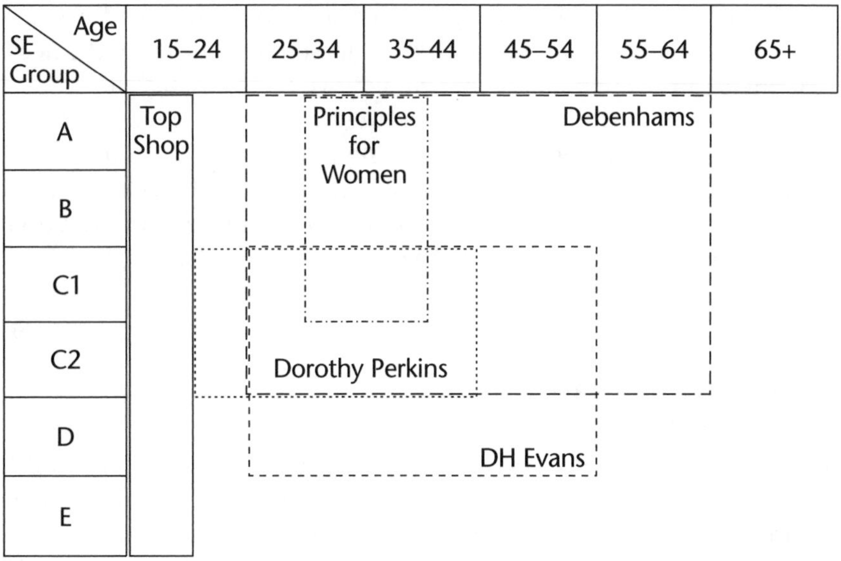

SE Group \ Age	15–24	25–34	35–44	45–54	55–64	65+
A	Top Shop	Principles for Women		Debenhams		
B						
C1						
C2		Dorothy Perkins				
D			DH Evans			
E						

Source: Burton Group *Annual Report*, 1993

Breaking your market into segments helps you to understand the composition of the market, interpret and present statistical information and target customers most likely to buy your products. Usually a market can be broken into segments by criteria such as age, occupation, home ownership, etc. When several criteria are applied, evidence can be produced of close relevance to the target market. For example, your product is a luxury which can only be afforded by certain income groups. Of these, you are only able to supply people in your immediate area. Of these, female homemakers are the main purchasers. They must be able to drive, be aged between 20 and 30 and have no children. It is not long before you have defined a quite precise group for whom a wide range of information is available.

Whatever the business's purpose, you should be specific regarding the segment in which you will operate. You might, for example:

■   offer bespoke software to large businesses; or

■   provide toys and games for children under 12 years old; or

■   provide an environmentally friendly range of packaging materials for use in the food industry.

Whilst it is important to understand your customers' needs, do not be totally constrained by what they tell you. Hamel and Prahalad (1994) point out that 'however well a company meets the articulated needs of current customers, it runs a great risk if it doesn't have a view of the needs customers can't yet articulate, but would love to have satisfied'.

It may be helpful to consider the values of your customers – what are they looking for in their suppliers, that is, you? They'll certainly be interested in quality, performance and delivery times. They'll probably be interested in your ability to innovate and improve. But they may also be interested in your business ethics.

Competitor analysis

There is little doubt that you will be better able to develop your business and achieve your goals if you have an understanding of your competitors. For most small businesses, there are likely to be many, many competitors and you clearly cannot assess all of them individually. But as you analyse the market place in general, you should also gain a feel for how your competitors see the market place. You can then group them together, depending on their approach to the market and the degree to which they are in direct competition. Some competitors may be more significant and you may want to look at them individually. This will require an understanding of the market place in which you are operating, and possibly also of the wider environment, which we will look at shortly.

It may help to pose questions around:

- Their customer *definition* – they may state it explicitly or you may be able to infer it from their activities.

- Their *strategies* for increasing sales – by further market penetration, perhaps, or by diversification.

- The *resources* that they have available.

What strategies are being followed by your competitors? What are their strengths and weaknesses? Do those represent threats or opportunities for you? In particular, ask yourself:

- What, precisely, are they selling and to whom?

- Is anyone doing this already?

- What do they charge?

- Are there gaps in the market?

- Is anyone likely to muscle in?

- What methods/equipment do they use?

- Are they any good at it and why?

Gathering information about your competitors is crucial, as this knowledge will play an important part in determining your strategy. You have to know everything about them: their product range, prices, discount structure, delivery arrangements, specifications, minimum order quantities, terms of trade and the kind of advertising that they use, where they advertise and with what success, what their customer profiling mix is and why customers buy from them.

Finding out information about your competitors may not be as difficult as it may seem. For instance, if you have experience within your market, you may already know a great deal about the competition. And you will probably know who you can talk to within the industry in order to find out more. Building up a number of contacts in your field will be useful for keeping up to date with what is happening in the market, and they can also be sources of advice.

Even if you are new to a particular market, there is a certain amount of information available to you. Trade journals are a useful source of information, with articles on your competitors and advertisements. If, in your market research with potential customers you talk to someone who is at present a customer of a competitor, they may be willing to tell you about the service they receive.

If your competitors are companies, they have to publish an annual report – these can be obtained from Companies House if they do not publish one formally. Gather copies of your competitors' marketing materials. Make sure that you have copies of their current price lists. Find out how they handle enquiries, what questions they ask, and what they perceive is important to their customers by their answers.

Finally, if you are feeling brave, you could talk to your competitors yourself (or get a friend to do it) and ask for brochures, sample quotes, or even purchase one of their products – particularly valuable if you are involved in manufacturing something that is not too expensive. Whether you admit to being a prospective or an actual competitor is up to you!

Reviewing the environment

Market places do not exist in isolation. As well as looking at customers, competitors and the market place, you also need to look more widely at the environment in which your business is operating and the likely environment in which it might be operating in, say, five years' time. You, and your business, need to learn as much as possible about the environment; furthermore you need to be sensitive to the demands and constraints of the environment. One of the characteristics of the current environment is that we are experiencing rapid change. And furthermore the rate of change appears to be increasing. This leads to uncertainty and consequently anxiety, even amongst people who are clearly successful. You can, however, reduce anxiety by analysing the environment and the changes that are taking place.

PEST analysis

One way of doing this is to undertake a PEST analysis.[1] Every business needs to consider a range of external forces in order to take decisions. For many people imagination is very limited and is coloured solely by their own experience and personal beliefs which can lead to wish fulfilment or a refusal to see reality or recognize the critical changes which are happening. It can also lead to rashly accepting short-term solutions which, if they do not exacerbate problems, certainly ignore the longer term. In the business world pressure is often applied to take decisions quickly acting on judgement and instinct rather than careful analysis.

There are many driving forces in the external environment which might impact on your business (Figure 2.3). These can be categorized as:

- social;

- technological;

- economic;

- environmental;

- political.

Social forces

Social forces include, for example, changing demography, education, etc. The population in western Europe is relatively static, but the age bands

FIGURE 2.3   Forces in the external environment

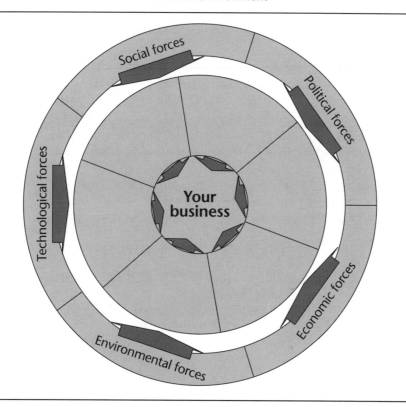

are changing. The number of older people, for example, is growing rapidly.

Within developed countries there is emerging a recognizable trend of individuals becoming more independently minded and critical with increased emphasis being placed on the free choice of the individual. One impact of this is that authority – be it in the form of employer, government, sovereign, church or parent – is no longer accepted without question. Individuals are more conscious of their rights and are often more determined to stand up for them. The spate of customer charters is one response to this and recognizes that individuals are increasingly exercising their rights as customers to choose and assert their individual tastes. Today, employees, particularly young people, are intolerant of close, hierarchical supervision. Employees, particularly the younger ones, want to be empowered to take responsibility for their own tasks, often working in small, well qualified teams. Companies are finding they can work very effectively in this way. In addition the younger generation are growing up in a global culture rather than the more restrictive and isolated cultures of earlier generations.

Many businesses now believe that location is less important than it once was. Modern communications make it easier to buy and sell abroad and so people are increasingly likely to base themselves where they want to live rather than where they have to work.

This willingness to do business abroad is likely to grow fast as the next generation of young people start in business, because of their experience of travelling abroad – and often of studying or working abroad – in much larger numbers than any previous generation. The world is becoming a smaller place and activities like the Internet mean that the English language is becoming increasingly dominant. In addition Music Television (MTV) is offering a Western culture to many more people. What effect, if any, might this have? Will English speakers become less inclined to learn foreign languages? Or will it matter less? Remember that the Germans say 'I will sell to you in any language, but I will only buy from you in German'.

Combine the liberation from location with the changes in 1990s lifestyles and values towards a greater emphasis on a balanced life – and is it too fanciful to imagine some clients locating where they can indulge their non-work interests? Students already expect to make greater use of computers in their studying – both for research and communicating with their tutors. Will this change the way that students study, perhaps spending more time away from school or university? Will it make school work more research oriented? What differences will come about as a result of them having to pay for tuition?

Think about population trends. You may need to have demographic features of your market included in your customer profiles, perhaps together with education bands and income distribution. What will be the effect of rapid population growth in some parts of the world such as China or India?

What do you think of your customers' concerns, motivations and attitudes regarding, for example, environmental issues, ethical issues, local issues, etc. What are their aspirations? Consumers are becoming increasingly concerned about the integrity and values of the businesses from whom they buy. Whilst this may, on the face of it, have less impact on the smaller business, be aware of the possible implications if you find yourself in a supply chain which serves larger businesses.

Technological forces

Technological forces are changing dramatically quickly. What effects will technological forces have on your production, marketing and distribution plans? Depending on your market, technology might either raise or lower entry barriers for competitors. Or it might completely change the industry as, for example, with the Swiss watch industry.

It is calculated, for example, that human scientific effort in 1992 alone was equal to all the scientific effort prior to 1960 (see Wybrew, 1992). Think back 10 or 15 years. Did you do your work on a personal computer? No. There were fewer than 10,000 PCs on the world's desktops a decade ago. By the turn of the century, there will be more than 180 million. Intel claims that since 1974, when the microprocessor first became available commercially, some 12 billion have been sold. Not only is their speed and computing power increasing dramatically, but they are also being used to control an extremely wide variety of functions. A BMW bought today has more computing power than the Apollo 11 moon rocket.

Ten years ago, how did you communicate with people? Via fax or electronic mail? Today, billions of dollars in commerce is conducted around the globe over fibre-optic cables. More and more people are gaining access to e-mail. This makes communications within businesses far easier too – it means all your staff can talk to you at any time. A company called Cisco make electronic switches for information and communication technology systems. Ten years ago they hardly existed – today they have a market capitalization bigger than General Motors. John Doerr, a particularly successful American venture capitalist states (Doerr, 1997) that during the 1980s, Silicon Valley was the site of the 'largest legal creation of wealth in the history of the planet'. In the UK, the telecom industry now employs twice as many people as the motor industry. Many now argue that advances in information and communication technology will be one of, if not the key, driving forces over the next 10 years or so. These advances will impact on many other activities. They enable companies to act more globally – for example moving work around the world in order to achieve the best value for money. Many more businesses, even small businesses, will find it easier to work across borders. This, in turn, may impact on distribution and supply arrangements and on greater liberalization of world trade. But it may also be affected by changing consumer values and by consumers benefiting from better communications – will consumers be willing to buy, say, footballs from factories in Asia exploiting child labour?

There has been an explosion of information. The last 30 years, for example, have seen a doubling of the information accumulated world-wide during the previous 5,000 years. And it is becoming ever easier to access – perhaps overwhelmingly so. It is estimated that just one day's *New York Times* contains more information than the average person of the seventeenth century absorbed in their entire lifetime! And the Internet and use of CD-ROMs is having a major impact on the transmission of information. Whilst there is little sign of it yet, we can expect reductions in the use of paper and far greater use of electronic transmission. *The Economist* now makes back issues available both on the Internet and on CD-ROM. Organizations like Key Note make all their market research reports available on CD-ROM. This makes them far easier to send through the post – and far easier to use. But what are the implications for printers? And for libraries? And will all the graphic designers be able to move quickly enough to the new medium? As Bill Gates (1994) has said, 'one thing about this revolution that's different from the PC revolution is that we think it's even bigger than the last one. And a lot of companies that will be huge players are ones you haven't heard of or that don't exist yet'.

Television technology, having been reasonably static since the advent of colour television, is now poised to make significant advances with the introduction of digital broadcasting and high definition television. This provides not only opportunities to sell new boxes – in the USA it has been estimated that 200 million sets will have to be replaced – but also opportunities for broadcasters. There are likely to be as many as 230 digital channels in the UK at the start of the next millennium.

It seems nothing is immune from the advance of electronics technology. Some of the most recent advances have been in digital photography. Casio, who did much to promote the advance of electronic calculators, are now leading the charge into developing ever better digital cameras. The quality still doesn't compete with traditional cameras – but they have opened up whole new markets for people wanting low resolution photographs, say for transmission by e-mail or for putting on the Internet. Who knows how quickly and how far the technology will develop over the next few years. Will traditional cameras go the way of analogue watches? And what new markets might be opened up by the new cameras?

The impact of information and communications technology is seen by everyone – and is coming into many more homes through rapid expansion of the Internet. But there are other new technologies which are advancing rapidly and which will have a major impact. These include, for example, ceramics (especially for use in high temperature applications such as car engines), robotics (leading to even less jobs in large manufacturers), fibre-optics (creating opportunities for narrowcasting and interactive television), biotechnology, genetic engineering and improved health care (leading to longer life expectancy and a greater demand on the welfare state in all Western countries).

There have been rapid advances in medical technology. Use of so-called key hole surgery means surgeons can operate inside you by remote control – but this also means that the surgeon can be in a totally different location, as is now occasionally happening. And virtual reality is offering doctors the chance to practise through simulations rather than on real patients.

Indeed, virtual reality is likely to offer many possibilities over the coming years as more people start to realize how it can be used to help them in their work – not just doctors, but anyone who currently might make use of models such as aircraft simulators and town planners. Government may also influence technology – through research spending for example.

Advancing technology may speed up the pace at which earlier technologies become obsolete, either because those technologies are no longer serviced or because everyone feels pressure to keep up with the pace of change (look at how the Pentium microprocessor displaced the 486, or the 486 displaced the 386).

The way you structure your office might change, utilizing advances in technology, because people are often away from the office, but with likely social consequences. Digital Equipment, for example, engages in 'hot desking' where staff can come in and use a desk, phone and computer – but there is an assumption that no more than half of the staff will be in at any one time. If lots of people are working out of the office, does the office need to become more of a meeting place, offering more social interaction? Video conferencing is already in use to reduce the need for travelling to meetings. This is likely to increase substantially as the technology improves and the cost reduces.

Economic forces

Economic forces include the effects of inflation, interest rates, tax rates, exchange rates and the Euro. Even governments have difficulty predicting what is likely to happen in these areas – and they try to control them! Nevertheless, they will have a major impact on your business, especially if you need to borrow a large proportion of your working capital, or if you are selling overseas.

The business environment is being transformed by global pressures. The Single European Market already has a population of 340 million people and a combined GDP of £2.5 trillion, larger than the USA and nearly twice Japan's. Think of all those potential customers – and it will expand further during the next 10 years.

Large cities can have a big impact on the economy. London, for example, is now estimated to have a GDP of $236bn – bigger than Belgium, Sweden and Austria – and nearly 20 per cent of the UK's GDP.

Even large companies can have a major impact on the world economy. The world's top 10 companies, for example, each have a turnover in excess of $100bn. General Motors' turnover is $160bn (Figure 2.4). Compare that to Britain's GDP of $1.3trn and they're not far behind and considerably higher than most countries' GDP.

Not surprisingly, companies can also have a big influence locally. Take Nissan for example. At their plant in Washington, Tyne and Wear, they have invested over £1.5bn and directly employ 4,000 people. But they have 55 suppliers located in the north east who collectively employ a further 25,000 people. And those suppliers have suppliers.

FIGURE 2.4 Comparison of countries by GDP and top companies by revenue

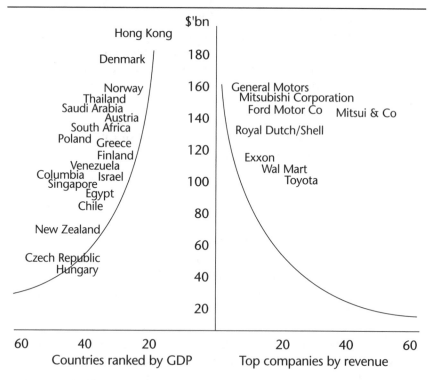

Sources: *The World in 1998*, Economist Publications; FT500, *Financial Times*, 22 January 1998

Much of the increase in the world economy over the next 30 years will occur in the developing world. Yet 94 per cent of SMEs in the UK do not export. Of those that do, only 4 per cent export more than 10 per cent of their total output. Unless your business is a local service business, you will undoubtedly face increasing competition from the rest of the EC. British companies have to compete for business in this global market place, selling and operating abroad and facing the growing competition of others in their home market. To succeed they must be as efficient as the best – which means reducing costs and organizing for utmost effectiveness. They must also offer a quality product or service. Increasingly discriminating consumers are putting much more pressure on all business to deliver high quality at low prices. Businesses will have to become more innovative to do this effectively.

What is happening further afield? African states are beginning to open their markets. China's economy is growing rapidly with a growth rate over 10 per cent per annum. On a purchasing power parity basis it now has the world's second largest economy. By 2010 some believe it will be the world's largest economy. Uruguay, Paraguay, Brazil and Argentina have created a common market called Mercosur adopting a common business language of Portuguese, creating a market of over $700bn and a combined population of over 200 million people.

Labour costs in central Europe and in the Third World will continue to be substantially lower than in the west – providing opportunities for low cost sub-contracting but also for overseas competitors potentially to undercut you.

By the middle of the twenty-first century a large part of the world's economy may well operate as a single market perhaps even with a single currency. Competition will increase, even in niche markets.

Think about the following:

- Interest rate trends for the next 12 months and how they will affect your cash flow and profitability.

- The sensitivity of your markets to interest rate fluctuations. Will customers buy less if interest rates rise, for example?

- Inflation rate for the products or services you sell and for the goods and services your business consumes and their impact on sales and profits.

- Exchange rate movements (even if you don't import directly, you may still be affected).

- Can increased costs be passed on to your customers without a marked effect on sales?

- Is your market(s) price sensitive?

- Is the economy prosperous: is expenditure stable, growing or declining?

- Unemployment trends amongst your customer groups.

- Who employs your customers and what is their financial state?

- Disposable income changes correlated with sales.

Are there factors very specific to your business? If you make maternity wear, what is happening to the birth rate? What will be the effect of women working longer before starting a family? Are there new markets into which you might diversify? Is your market growing or contracting or static? How many competitors do you have? What new markets are opening up?

A young person starting off as a jobbing builder specializing in house improvements and extensions, for example, may be affected by:

- mortgage rates: if they are high, more people may prefer to keep their current house and improve rather than move;

- DIY popularity;

- unemployment levels: if they are high in the area, it means that there is more free time for people to do their own repairs, that they have less money to pay others to do the work, and that there may be more competitors in the 'informal economy'.

Leisure is becoming an increasingly important part of people's time, but it is also providing many more business opportunities. The music industry, in the UK, is estimated to be worth £2.5bn – versus £2.4bn for the water industry.

Environmental forces

Environmental forces are becoming increasingly important as more people consider the consequences of continually interfering with the ecological balance of nature. As a result, governments are legislating more to protect the environment and demanding less pollution. Some are introducing special requirements, for example, demanding that all packaging must be recycled. Whilst there is inevitably a higher initial cost to meeting such requirements, there may be a long-term pay off as the business wastes less and meets consumer demand more closely. There may also be opportunities to assist other businesses to meet their requirements.

Food safety and nutrition are likely to become even bigger issues than they are now. It is estimated that there are now over three million vegetarians with 5,000 people every week becoming vegetarian, many citing the BSE scare as the main reason. There is growing concern over the effect of intensive farming on the environment, and a greater desire for organic produce.

Identify the consumer or environmental pressure groups that might influence your markets. Are you aware of any plans in the pipeline for new housing, commercial, road transport and other developments which will affect your markets and/or product distribution?

Political forces

Political forces most obviously include legislation passed by governments, forcing businesses to comply, for example, with health and safety, or employment, or data protection requirements. These impose costs upon business, but they often also provide opportunities.

For most of the twentieth century the world appeared quite simply to be divided into two major forces for development. On the one hand there was capitalism with its class society, a concentration of private ownership companies and the free market operating. On the other hand, there was socialism, with its classless society, state ownership, powerful trade unions, nationalization of companies and overwhelming control through central planning. The third world as it became known was a diversion for the two systems, capitalism and communism to fight over – territories to perpetuate the best and worst of each.

Then came *perestroika* in the Soviet Union, the end of the threat of the Cold War, Solidarity's victory in Poland, reunification of Germany – the collapse of communism in Eastern Europe followed by great political and social unrest and uncertainty in many former communist countries and alliances. The end of the Cold War released a wide variety of nationalist sentiment which had been suppressed for many years and, as in the former Yugoslavia, may result in regional conflicts causing great destruction. In other areas, economic uncertainties have replaced the threat once posed by military force.

A vacuum has been created in many instances with the collapse of one system followed by a rush to import ready made solutions from the other system in the West. The emerging democracies in central and eastern Europe are all eager to join the European Union which will probably become less of a Union as a result and more of a Community. The enormous market thus created will provide many more opportunities – for export, for import, for sub-contracting, for joint ventures, for technology transfer, etc.

The reduction of the threat of global warfare will create opportunities and challenges. The spread of free market economies has brought east and west to the point where they face the same kind of both economic and social problems. Environmental and welfare issues and concerns will increasingly have an impact through legislation and consumer pressure providing both constraints and opportunities for business.

Many small businesses may feel that political forces are unlikely to affect their business. If you are one of those, think about the following possible changes in legislation which may affect you and your business:

- product design and safety regulations;

- product description labelling and packaging;

- product guarantees;

- trade practices and regulating bodies;

- retail trading hours;

- pricing;

- advertising practice;

- employment legislation;

- minimum wage regulations.

Networking

A study in America implies that every American is linked to any other American – through friends, colleagues or relatives – by just five links. That is, I have a friend who knows a colleague who has a relative who has a pal who knows Bill Clinton. Well, not quite! But Americans are notorious for their networking. They all have their Rolodex of contacts and telephone numbers. Be like them.

Arguably, the people who now do best are not those with the best ideas or the brightest minds. They are the ones with the best contacts –

ideally in different networks – and who are happy to exploit those contacts.

Let me give an example. Recently, I have been assisting a client raise finance for a joint venture in the Czech Republic. I assisted in setting up the national Risk Capital Fund. Someone I know set up a Regional Equity Fund in the very region in which my client plans to locate. And a friend of a friend is Chief Executive of an Austrian bank's Czech subsidiary.

Network widely – join organizations, such as Rotary Clubs which have traditionally been seen as a fertile ground for networking purposes, or your local Chamber of Commerce or professional institutes such as the Institute of Management or Institute of Directors – where you can meet other people involved in business and the local community. Keep a note of names and telephone numbers – your address book should be your most important asset. Management guru, Rosabeth Moss-Kanter (1997), from the Harvard Business School, points out in her book, *World Class* that the most successful companies are those with the three Cs:

- concepts;

- competences;

- connections.

This has been translated as the best ideas, the best skills and the best Rolodex.

Networking is important when you are working, or considering working, internationally. You have to make an effort to discover key people locally – and to use those people to your advantage. It is particularly important in Asia – where companies believe that the relationship comes first and business opportunities are secondary, unlike the Western approach of identifying a business opportunity and then seeking and activating the connection to exploit it.

Networking is the active cultivation of useful contacts and the use of those contacts, when appropriate, to help in achieving required objectives. In most cases, those objectives are locating information and finding new customers. It is unusual to be in the fortunate position of having a directory of willing contacts provided, but even without such a starting point, building a good network of contacts is something that can be achieved over time.

Research can be conducted through careful use of contacts to establish whether a market is viable in the first place. Whatever your position in a market you will want to be aware of any developments that might indirectly affect your business; a network can help here too. The right people can provide you with information about proposed changes in legislation in your industry, problems faced by customers or suppliers (or your customers' customers and suppliers' suppliers), etc. that might have a knock-on effect on your business.

Networking is something that a lot of people do without ever thinking about it, but if it is carried out as a deliberate activity it is much easier to control the results. Chance encounters should never be ignored. Every conversation or introduction has the potential to provide useful contacts.

Seek out places where useful contacts might gather. Your local enterprise agency may know of, or organize, an enterprise club. Enterprise clubs provide a relatively informal setting for people who run small businesses to get together socially, arrange entertainment and educational programmes, etc. Local Chambers of Commerce usually hold regular informal meetings for members, often based around informative talks followed by a buffet lunch. Don't be afraid to introduce yourself to people and discuss what both you and they do.

There may also be other fora which are specific to your industry or current business interests, for example regional branches of your trade association, professional institutions such as the Institute of Management, exporters' clubs, etc. These are usually designed specifically for the purpose of establishing contacts and exchanging information. And don't forget any social or community activities in which you are involved.

Look for intermediaries who can make introductions. The professionals that you deal with in business life are also dealing with other businesses. If you need to find contacts in a particular area try asking your accountant, solicitor or bank manager. Although they will be unable to discuss other clients in detail they may be able to make referrals.

Don't forget friends – and friends of friends. Most people have a variety of friends, relatives and acquaintances, who in turn have their own circle of friends, etc. Within this comparatively close set of relationships it is astonishing how often you know somebody who knows somebody who can help – the difficulty lies in making the initial connection.

Aim for a core of around seven or eight key people with whom you constantly exchange information. In addition, keep regular contact with the rest of your main contacts – you will have to determine the frequency appropriate to each. Many people make use of fax or e-mail to maintain their networks, regularly circulating relevant information between contacts. Some contacts can be noted down for future reference without a need to keep in touch. Inevitably, such contacts are more likely to fall out of date, but if you didn't need to get in touch with them for a long time you haven't wasted any effort.

Communication is the key; if you let people know what you are doing, what sort of information you need, etc., they will be better placed to help you than if you keep yourself to yourself. Be prepared to work at networking. If you want to get the most out of it you have to put a lot into it. If you expect people to feed you information you should be prepared to feed information to others. If you are in the habit of passing news on without being asked, others might learn to do the same for you.

Benchmarking

So far, this chapter has concentrated entirely on looking at the market place and the environment to identify opportunities and threats. There is, however, another very good reason to look around outside your business. Engage in what Tom Peters (1987) calls 'creative swiping' or David Garvin (1993) calls 'enthusiastic borrowing'. Larger businesses have systemized this into benchmarking – which is simply a way of assessing your business by comparing yourself with the best practice in other firms. It involves understanding, analysing and learning from their systems and quality practices, identifying the most efficient and effective approaches and applying them to your own business. Specifically, look at the functions in your own business – and then look at the way other businesses undertake these same functions. How can you improve what you do? Do not be afraid of looking at what other businesses are doing. You might be able to use what you learn to become more efficient or more effective. Benchmarking will help you to assess your performance in a particular area relative to the organization with which you are comparing yourself. Do not attempt to compare too many areas at once. Concentrate on the one or two where you may already consider yourself to be weak. Don't restrict yourself just to looking at what businesses similar to yourself do. Look at those businesses that are the best in the particular activity you want to improve. Southwest Airlines, for example, in trying to be a low cost airline, was concerned that its aeroplanes were on the ground too long between flights, largely due to the time required to refuel. Having benchmarked itself against other airlines, and concluded it was already ahead of the game, it then compared itself against the fastest – Formula One racing cars – and, as a result, was able to reduce its own refuelling time substantially.

The University of Northumbria, working closely with the CBI, and building on work by IBM and the London Business School, has developed a tool called PILOT which provides an introduction to benchmarking.

The business completes a questionnaire and gets results in the form of two graphs as illustrated in Figures 2.5 and 2.6.

The scatter graph in Figure 2.5 positions organizations on scales of practice and performance relating to world class standards and gives an overall comparison with the rest of the sample. The university suggests that those in the bottom left quadrant could do better – they are low in both best practice and performance leaving plenty of scope to increase their competitiveness. Those in the bottom right quadrant are promising, show good practice though this has not yet shown up in their performance, possibly due to a lack of focus or a concentration on less appropriate practices. Those in the top left are performing well but could be vulnerable to market or wider environmental pressures because of their low use of best practice. Winning businesses, appearing in the top right quadrant demonstrate best practice and good performance. Focusing effort on their weakest areas may help to move further still towards the top right hand corner where you might reasonably regard yourself as world class.

The bar chart in Figure 2.6, which assesses six business aspects, compares the business's performance to other similar businesses. The bar shows the range for the four quartiles (that is, one quarter of the

FIGURE 2.5 Scatter graph of performance vs. practice

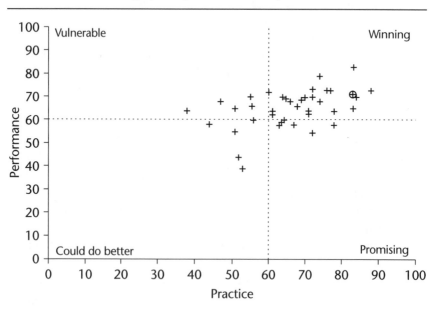

FIGURE 2.6   Bar chart comparison against other businesses

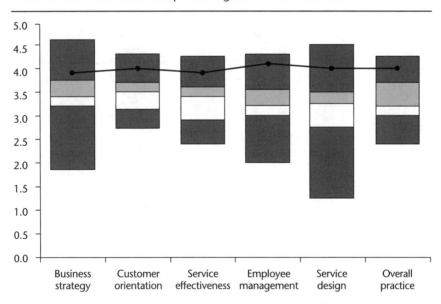

businesses in the sample fall within the ranges shown); the line shows the result for Project North East, the organization for which I work.

As so often with business analysis, it is not so much the results that are important – indeed, good results can have the wrong effect of leading to complacency – but the process. It is by asking the questions, and thinking about the implications, that businesses can begin to consider better ways of doing things. The bar chart may help to prioritize where the effort is required.

The University of Northumbira has developed a more sophisticated tool, called PROBE, which will provide a deeper analysis. Alternatively, you may find the EFQM model helpful (Figure 2.7).

Since 1992, the European Foundation for Quality Management (EFQM) has made awards to companies who can demonstrate excellence in their management of quality.

The EFQM model has been deliberately designed to encourage businesses to look at all aspects of their performance and to engage in a process of self-analysis. Specifically, the model suggests that leadership drives policy and strategy, staff management and resource management ensuring that the right processes are in place to achieve staff satisfaction, customer satisfaction and impact on society. If these aspects are properly achieved they lead to excellence in business results. Their model can be

FIGURE 2.7 EFQM model

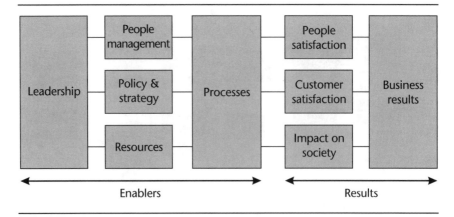

used to provoke questions when considering strengths and weaknesses – which we look at in Chapter Four – but also when considering what others are doing. Use the model to benchmark yourself against other businesses.

Xerox, one of the pioneers of benchmarking, have a step by step approach: plan (identify the benchmarking subject, identify companies with which to compare, decide on the data to be collected), analyse (measure the gap, look at the trends), integrate (share the results, set goals) and act (agree an action plan, implement the plan, monitor, recalibrate).

For your benchmarking to be effective, you need to think carefully about what it is that you intend to look at. You could start with one of your key business objectives and then use a cause and effect diagram to identify the processes in your business that will effect your chosen business objective. If, for example, you are interested in customer satisfaction, think about everything that might support or harm your ability to satisfy customers, which I have defined as delivering a product or service, of the agreed quality, at the agreed price, at the time specified (Figure 2.8).

Gathering market intelligence

There is a tremendous amount of information available about what is happening in the wider environment and in your market place. Read the

FIGURE 2.8 Cause and effect diagram

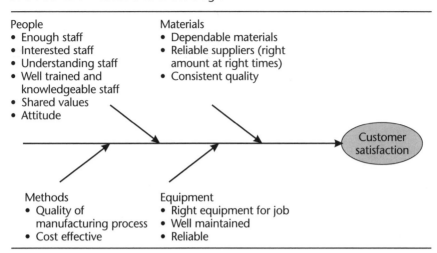

People
- Enough staff
- Interested staff
- Understanding staff
- Well trained and knowledgeable staff
- Shared values
- Attitude

Materials
- Dependable materials
- Reliable suppliers (right amount at right times)
- Consistent quality

Customer satisfaction

Methods
- Quality of manufacturing process
- Cost effective

Equipment
- Right equipment for job
- Well maintained
- Reliable

business pages in the newspapers; read *The Economist* – if you can afford it, subscribe to the Economist Intelligence Unit country reports or business reports; surf the Internet – it is amazing how much valuable information is quickly and easily available. In short, keep an eye on what is happening. Be a squirrel. Horde the information. Set up a filing system so it is easily accessible. Or exploit modern technology – I now scan interesting articles and store them on computer so they are easily available when I want to refer to them.

It is essential that management decisions are based on appropriate information. You need to know about employee performance, and how the business is performing, if you are to control and improve operations adequately. Information about competitors, markets and technology is essential for strategic planning. Too often information is gathered and used in an *ad hoc* fashion. Information can be inadequate, or there can be far too much of it. Some businesses are more 'information critical' than others. It helps to see information management as a distinct function, to budget for it and to manage it in order to achieve maximum effectiveness. Big companies reach a high level of sophistication in this area, but even small operations will benefit from a more systematic approach.

Information should not be confused with data. A list of figures means little without explanation. To be useful, data must be turned into information by analysing it and presenting it in a form appropriate to the user.

In smaller businesses, managers stay aware of market conditions through their daily contact with customers and suppliers. As the business grows, managers become ever more distant from the grass roots and do not have immediate access to this basic information. A senior manager may be too busy to check personally on every aspect of the operation, but still needs to know what is happening in order to make valid strategic decisions. There comes a time when a separate information resource should be introduced to the business.

Information management is about finding a way to collect, handle and distribute information to the right people. Good information is relevant, accurate, and produced at the required time. Data must be collected, stored, analysed and presented to managers in an appropriate form. There should be a strategy to ensure that the correct information is received, and that any held is not kept too long nor is it thrown out earlier than legal requirements allow. It should ensure that the information is presented appropriately, and that it can be retrieved when the need arises.

Staff should be involved in developing the information strategy. Information gathering activities should be co-ordinated. In some firms people collect data independently and do not pass it on to colleagues. They may not realize its importance to other sections of the business or may be trying to protect their own jobs. If everyone realizes the importance of information to the whole company, the strategy may be more successful. Produce a written document including objectives, policy, budgets, responsibilities and any other relevant documentation (e.g. lists of categories, request forms, etc.). Ensure staff know how to use the system.

- Ensure that staff at all levels know the importance of information as a business resource.

- Information must be circulated to the right people, and in a useful format.

- Management information can be a sensitive issue. Be aware of this and try to ensure that the development of a system does not create internal political squabbles.

- Any information system you develop should be as simple as possible; if everyone can understand it, it is less likely to go wrong.

Attracting resources

You will only be able to implement your strategy if you have, or can attract, the required resources – human, physical and financial.

At an early stage in developing your strategy, you will need to decide whether you are willing to seek support from venture capitalists – people or organizations willing to provide equity capital in exchange for shares in your business. Many entrepreneurs resist venture capital on the grounds that they do not want to lose control or that they want to own 100 per cent. I would argue, on the other hand, that having 50 or 60 or 70 per cent of a very large business is better than having 100 per cent of a very small business. Richard Onians (1995) argues strongly that businesses, instead of relying on debt finance, should seek sufficient equity to enable the business to reach the stage where it is generating cash. In particular, he notes that loan finance should only be considered if the interest can be comfortably afforded out of earnings. Arie de Geus (1997) makes a similar point in his book, *The Living Company* when he notes that long lived companies are conservative in their financing, understanding that spare cash offers flexibility to pursue opportunities when they arise.

You only have to look at some of the big successes, particularly but not exclusively in the USA, of businesses started from nothing which have grown big with assistance from third party equity. These include Microsoft, Intel, Compaq, Apple, Sun Microsystems, Lotus, Netscape and Amazon.com.

Most venture capitalists do want to see their stake grow, and to make a decent profit eventually. But they also recognize that they cannot rush the process. Instead, they are likely to provide considerable support to nurture the firm and, often, inject additional capital should it be required during early growth.

Opportunities and threats

Draw up a SWOT matrix as in Figure 2.9. But don't just do it once, use it as a regular management tool, updating it as you spot opportunities or learn more about the market place.

After reading this chapter, you should be able to make a good start at filling it in. Opportunities and threats are external. What threats, if any, do you conclude from your competitor analysis? Are there any gaps, or niche markets, not being served by your competitors – do these offer opportunities?

What opportunities and threats arise from your PEST analysis? Does rapidly advancing technology give you the opportunity to enter a new market? Or does the Internet provide the means to seek new customers?

FIGURE 2.9 SWOT analysis

Strengths	Weaknesses
Opportunities	Threats

Or will opening markets in central Europe, with lower labour costs, pose a threat?

External influences affect the strategy and your ability both to fulfil your purpose and to achieve your vision. The market place clearly presents a series of opportunities and threats – opportunities to identify new customer groups and different customer needs but threats from competitors and changes in the way your customers' needs can be addressed. The availability of extra resources may be an opportunity though many businesses find that resource availability is a large constraint.

Once you have a list of opportunities and threats, you will want to consider how to exploit the opportunities (if at all) and how to avoid the threats. Exploiting the opportunities may help you think about long-term goals and we will return to this later.

Strengths and weaknesses are internal, though looking outwards, in a benchmarking analysis for example, will help you to assess your strengths and weaknesses.

How well do you compare? Your assessment will include aspects such as production efficiency, technological capabilities, financial strength, distribution capabilities, etc. These are internal factors related to how well your business is able to perform relative to your competitors. You also need to look at yourself from the viewpoint of your customers. They are unlikely to be particularly concerned about whether your production process is more efficient than a competitor's or whether you have more up to date equipment. They are much more likely to base their view of your strengths and weaknesses on factors such as speed of response, standards of customer care, product quality issues and perceived value for money – the issues that matter to them.

As with the opportunities and threats, you then need to consider how you will build on your strengths and address or eliminate your weaknesses.

Conclusion

In this chapter we have looked at what is happening now, or in the near future, and have started the process of understanding the strengths, weaknesses, opportunities and threats. It has been emphasized that this should be a continuous process rather than a one-off exercise. It is essential that you look out from your business – to understand the environment and the market place, to profit your customers, to analyse your competitors, to use business networks and to benchmark your own performance.

Note

1 This is sometimes known now as a STEEP analysis, adding an extra E for the environment. Bob Garratt (1996) refers to PPESTT analysis, adding an extra physical (that is, environment) and an extra T for trade forces.

CHAPTER THREE

Looking ahead

Crystal balls

Looking at your market place and looking at the environment will tell you a great deal about the current position. But you also need to look for trends and likely changes in the future. It is impossible to predict with any degree of accuracy what will happen – yet it is becoming increasingly important to have at least an idea of what the future might hold in order both to set goals and to have a chance of attaining them. Inevitably what we do is guided by what has happened, or what we think has happened previously, by our assumptions and perception of the present and by our best guess of what will happen in the future. Some trends and possible changes can be gleaned from your PEST analysis, some may require more effort. Your analysis should however help you to identify the likely drivers of change. This chapter explains two techniques that may be helpful in looking ahead; the results of that forward review can be used to expand on the list of opportunities and threats developed in the last chapter. The chapter concludes by introducing the idea of impact analysis – what will be the impact of possible changes on you and your competitors.

Once you start to think more about the future, you will find that it does not require a lot of extra effort. It simply requires a greater awareness. So much of what we see around us depends on having had our consciousness raised about some particular topic. It's probably happened to you. You decide to change your car. Let's say you're interested in a Renault Megane. All of a sudden you start noticing different models – the standard saloon, different engine options, the sporty version, the scenic – driving round the streets. They were still there before, but you didn't notice them, because there was no reason to trigger any response. But as soon as your consciousness is raised, then you start to notice.

Foresight

The way we act in a particular situation is based on our interpretation of what has happened previously, assumptions about the present and our expectations of the future. If the same thing keeps happening, and the market response is always the same, then we can be lulled into a false sense of security.

Having foresight is not the same as having second sight: it is not about predicting the future. Foresight is simply being aware of what is happening in your market place and in the wider environment and having some ideas about what might happen – to be useful, of course, you also need to have an idea of how you might respond.

Having foresight means that

- you will have a better idea of likely future influences and triggers both on the market in which you are operating and on your particular business and be able to anticipate change;

- you will identify possible trends and future events which may impact on your business, perhaps enabling you to identify and fill new customer needs;

- you will be more likely to make, and retain, contact with people and organizations who are attempting to identify those trends, widening your network and giving you advance notice of both opportunities and threats;

- you are able to look further into the future giving more time to assess your possible response and, if necessary, to reconsider your strategic direction.

In trying to be foresightful, you will need to make some assumptions – based on your PEST analysis – of what is likely to continue as it is and of what is likely to change. The occasional brainstorming session, or Delphi analysis, may help here. It is important to remember, however, that you need to think through the implications of the driving forces that you identified in your PEST analysis. Most analyses are static ones, describing the relevant forces at any instant in time. You are interested in the forces months or years hence. This may present particular problems if there are major changes, or discontinuities, taking place.

A major change took place in the computer industry some years ago. The advent of the microprocessor and Microsoft's operating system resulted in computers being suddenly transformed from high cost, differentiated products to low cost commodities. New applications – like

Lotus 1-2-3 – gave many more people reasons to want to have a computer. The cost of entry plummeted and new companies, like Compaq and Dell, came from nowhere almost overnight. Those who could foresee ways in which people could use computers – Netscape is a recent example – and write relevant software have done very well.

In a Delphi analysis a panel of people with some appropriate expertise are surveyed by written questionnaire – start with your staff, and your customers and suppliers if they are willing to co-operate. The results of the questionnaire are circulated to all of the panellists together with a revised questionnaire. The objective is to forecast what might happen under particular circumstances, whilst eliminating effects such as majority opinion by having everyone together in a group. A Delphi analysis might typically be used to forecast what might happen after the launch of a new product, or for the likely effects of new technologies. It is used when other research methods cannot be applied and is usually fairly accurate when looking at the medium to long term.

Make sure that you talk to and involve those who are 'closest to the coal-face'. The staff who are closest to your customers – probably your sales people or your middle managers – are likely to be most attuned to possible change (see Grove, 1997). They will have considerable knowledge but may have a relatively narrow focus, so their views need to be balanced by the wider perspective of senior managers.

After Netscape developed their Navigator software, allowing for the first time anyone to access the internet, Microsoft failed to believe the world wide web would have any real impact. Yet it took off – because of user demand – and Microsoft had to work hard to get back in the race.

Having thought about the changes, you can then construct pictures of possible futures – scenarios. And you can use those models to think about how you might respond. What choices do you have? Is there anything that you can do now – just in case? Are there new opportunities?

In trying to become more foresightful you are not entirely on your own. In 1993 the government launched its own 'Foresight Programme'. This resulted in the setting up of the sector specific panels, consultations with over 10,000 people and the publication of reports outlining the change drivers and likely social, economic and market trends which were thought likely to influence business over the next 20 years or so. In addition, they have identified a mind-blowing 1200 topics – covering scientific and technological advances, market information and policy issues.

These are topics which the panels think merit investigation for new business opportunities. They have attempted to rate them by attractiveness and feasibility (Figure 3.1). Those that are most attractive have been described as being priority areas. They have also described their view of

FIGURE 3.1

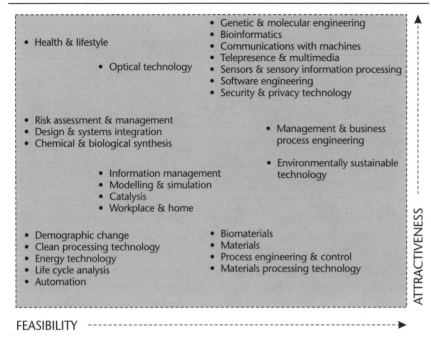

- Health & lifestyle

- Optical technology

- Genetic & molecular engineering
- Bioinformatics
- Communications with machines
- Telepresence & multimedia
- Sensors & sensory information processing
- Software engineering
- Security & privacy technology

- Risk assessment & management
- Design & systems integration
- Chemical & biological synthesis

- Management & business process engineering

- Environmentally sustainable technology

- Information management
- Modelling & simulation
- Catalysis
- Workplace & home

- Demographic change
- Clean processing technology
- Energy technology
- Life cycle analysis
- Automation

- Biomaterials
- Materials
- Process engineering & control
- Materials processing technology

ATTRACTIVENESS

FEASIBILITY

Source: 'Progress Through Partnership: Report from the Steering Group', Office of Science and Technology

the opportunities. If you are working in any of these areas, then buying or borrowing the relevant report could well assist you in thinking about possible future developments.

Having made a stab at being foresightful may tell you something about the future environment, but you need to think carefully about the implications for your business. Indeed, starting from a requirement for a business decision makes sense.

Impact analysis

The factors you have identified in your PEST analysis as likely to influence your market place and the environment may impact differently on different businesses, reflecting their own particular strengths and weaknesses. If you have good intelligence about some of your competitors you may find it helpful to undertake an impact analysis (Table 3.1).

TABLE 3.1

External influences	Businesses		
	Us	Competitor A	Competitor B
Internationalization/ globalization of business	Poor foreign language skills	Uses language bureau	Excellent foreign language skills
Ease of international travel	Willing to market internationally but little spare cash	Use agents	Happy to jump on plane – encroaching into our market
Increasing demand for certification to ISO9000	Already have it	Working towards it	Apparently not interested

An impact analysis helps to structure what you know about your competitors, but, by itself, doesn't tell you much about what they might do in a given situation, or how they might react to external forces.

Rehearsing the future

You probably think through dozens of 'what if. . .' questions every day. You may only think ahead a few minutes or a few hours. 'If I go into the showroom to look at the Megane, the salesman will ask if he can help me – what will I say'; 'the salesman will ask if I have a trade-in – how much do I tell him I want for it'; 'If there's fog at the airport, can I catch the train instead?' These are not predictions, they are scenarios. We store the answers – Arie de Geus (1997) refers to them as 'memories of the future' – and then, if a particular future unfolds, we already know what we are going to do, so we just do it. Thinking about the future, and thinking about responses, enables us to be prepared. As Arie de Geus suggests, 'we would have thought about our course and planned it out in our imagination. We would not have to try to predict the future, because we could rely on our memory of the many futures that we have already visited.' Scenarios can assist in identifying decisions that may have to be taken in the future, particularly decisions that might otherwise be missed.

Scenario planning

As with so many of the techniques used in strategic planning, the use of scenarios first appeared after the Second World War as an aid to assist the United States Air Force to imagine what their enemies might do under certain circumstances and, more importantly, to plan their response.

Scenario planning helps organizations to build models of the future which reflect the real world and which are shared and accepted by the organization's management team. Preparing scenarios can be particularly helpful in identifying key features of the business environment, including opportunities and threats. Whilst changes may be obvious, especially demographic changes, the implications of those changes may be rather less obvious. Scenario planning can be used both to look generally at what might happen in the environment (for example, the effect on the economy if the government changes) and to help you think specifically about your own business within the environment. Scenario planning is a way of helping organizations consider what they already know or can easily discover about the possible environment in which they will be working, say, five years ahead. It helps to add a framework to the process of strategic thinking. Scenarios are not forecasts – they simply reflect one possible way in which the future might emerge. It makes sense, therefore, to consider two or three scenarios, that is, two or three plausible views of the future. Hopefully, scenarios will assist in the process of understanding the dynamics of change. The thinking process will highlight factors which can have a high impact but which are also highly uncertain. When you understand the possible changes, and can put them in context, you are in a far better position to protect yourself against possible threats.

Case study: Shell

Shell UK Ltd, in particular, has pioneered the use of scenario planning in business. They are particularly proud of one scenario, set out in 1984. The price of oil was $28 a barrel; one scenario envisaged oil falling to $16 a barrel by April 1986. With some pushing, Shell executives devised plans to address this possible scenario. As it happened the price of oil did fall: from $27 in January 1986 to $17 in February and just $10 in April. The fact that Shell had already considered what it would do helped considerably during that period (see Geus, 1988).

Another story from Shell, told by Peter Schwartz (1992), demonstrates the effectiveness of scenario planning. In 1983, Yuri Andropov had just come to power in the USSR. Ronald Reagan and Margaret Thatcher continued to reiterate their Cold War rhetoric. Mikhail Gorbachev was an obscure official in the Communist Party. Shell was reviewing demand for North Sea gas and considering whether to develop the Troll gas field. The platform and associated equipment would cost over $6bn and sell natural gas to the whole of Europe. The other potential supplier of natural gas was the Soviet Union – and they could provide it far cheaper. For obvious reasons, the Europeans had agreed informally to limit supplies from the Soviet Union to 35 per cent of the market. Shell were concerned, however, that it would take a long time and cost a great deal of money to develop this new gas field. To be worthwhile, Shell needed a decent return on their investment – and to get that return, they needed decent sales. What, they asked themselves, might affect those sales?

The planners therefore asked under what circumstances might there be a change to the artificially imposed limit on the USSR of a 35 per cent market share. In other words what might make the USSR change sufficiently for the West to reduce or remove the limit. The planners concluded that a failing Soviet economy might force the USSR to change away from its rigid system. The planners also concluded that the Soviet economy was failing.

One of the scenarios they developed (the Greening of Russia) postulated Gorbachev achieving power, massive economic and political restructuring, opening to the West, declining tension in the West, and major shifts in international relationships.

It is important, however, to remember two things. First, Gorbachev did not cause the changes in the USSR; his achievement of power was a symptom of the underlying causes. Second, Shell did not forecast that this would happen. It was simply one possible view of the future, which they used in their decision making process. As with the fall in oil prices, this was not a forecast. It was prepared to help Shell understand the environment in which they operated and what might stimulate major changes.

When preparing scenarios, Shell build in sufficient milestones in order to identify which one is unfolding. In other words, what will be the key developments within each scenario? The milestones will assist in recognizing which scenario is occurring. This is essential if it is to be an effective tool in your planning process.

Scenario planning can be productively utilized by small businesses as well as large ones. Peter Schwartz, in *The Art of The Long View* (1997), explains that the key is to define the driving forces, the predetermined elements and the critical uncertainties all of which have considerable overlap.

The ideal scenarios are prepared to help with a key decision, as with Shell's question about investing in the Troll gas platform, or whether you should start a business or launch a new product. You need, therefore, to consider the driving forces appropriate to your decision. Driving forces might include demographics, level and cost of imports (of competing products), changing technology, etc. Schwartz looks for driving forces under the five categories mentioned earlier in the PEST analysis: society, technology, economics, politics and environment. Technological change will usually have the biggest impact, because the change is so fast and can be so great. So look for likely changes in technology. Peter Schwartz recommends looking elsewhere – music, for example, often encapsulates the feelings of society, before those feelings begin to have a major impact. And look outside your usual environment. Read widely. Talk to people. Surf the Internet.

Predetermined elements are those that can be predicted accurately because they change very slowly (such as demography), are tightly constrained or are already in the pipeline. For example, if you are selling to people aged 18–25 (like night clubs) then you are targeting a declining market – but the size of the market and the way it will change is known in advance. Similarly, the consumption of items such as food only changes slowly.

Critical uncertainties need to be explored carefully. Your actions will depend on the 'what ifs' you pose. What if . . . tax rates change? (more disposable income? less disposable income?) What if . . . consumers have more disposable income? (less DIY? more DIY?) What if . . . costs of transmitting local television by cable fall dramatically? (scope for more local TV? use of TV by narrow interest groups?) What if . . . local authorities put more of their services out to private businesses? If, for example, interest rates rise what effect will that have on mortgages and, in turn, on disposable income? Will customers be likely to stop spending on certain non-essential items – like paying others to do repairs, painting and decorating? Or will they be less likely to move – and spend more on repairs, painting and decorating? Will they do more themselves – increasing the level of DIY sales?

What will the effect be, for example, of increasing numbers of cars on Britain's roads? One outcome might be that the Chancellor keeps on putting up the price of fuel, resulting in people buying much smaller, more economical cars. This will make it harder for them to carry bulky items (say, for all their DIY purchases), so there may be opportunities for cheap, efficient, local transport businesses. Another outcome might be that people spend even more time stuck in traffic jams and look for better in-car hi-fi systems. Or more people may decide to abandon their cars in favour of public transport. Tax is almost always a critical uncertainty. What happens when the Chancellor makes unexpected changes like removing the tax relief for the elderly on private health insurance?

Scenario planning helps businesses to build models of the future which reflect the real world and which are shared and accepted by the business's management team. Scenarios do not have to be complicated or elaborate. Indeed, for a smaller business you should aim to keep them as simple as possible. And in many ways it is the process of thinking that is more important. As you might expect, if the key members of staff, usually the management team, are involved in researching and preparing the scenarios, it is more likely that there will be mutual ownership. Furthermore, the preparation will be particularly helpful in identifying key features in the business environment, including opportunities and threats. Do not develop too many scenarios. Aim for no more than two or three. Give them names so that you can refer to them easily. Scenarios will help you to replace uncertainty with understanding. An external facilitator may be helpful both in preparing the scenarios and in developing responses. If possible, involve some of your key stakeholders – perhaps a major customer. Do they share your analysis?

Case Study: Agency for the Development of Enterprise, Sevastopol

Background

The ADE is an initiative based in Kiev in Ukraine intended to assist entrepreneurs to start and grow businesses. In early 1997, it opened an office in Sevastopol. Their key source of finance, at the time of the study, was EC aid through a programme known as TACIS. The description and scenarios were prepared by the author as part of a consultancy assignment intended to highlight specific needs and to suggest how those needs could be fulfilled.

Sevastopol ADE has made an excellent start. In just eight months, they have recruited and trained staff, attracted nearly 300 clients and provided a high number of training courses. They have integrated themselves into the local community and are looking more widely at the scope for working throughout Crimea.

Green shoots

TACIS financial support is not only retained, but also expanded, enabling the agency to recruit and train additional staff. This will allow the agency to offer more training and counselling not only in Sevastopol but throughout Crimea. That TACIS support makes it very worthwhile for the UK government's Know How Fund to continue to provide technical assistance – and those two together give confidence to other donors, such as Soros and Eurasia, who agree to support other, more ambitious developments. This provides a first step in reducing dependence on any single funding source.

These developments include the establishment of a loan fund, initially on a pilot basis, but subsequently growing with funding from TACIS '97, the development and management of an incubator workspace, which will provide non-grant dependent income to the agency, and the introduction of additional consultancy and training services, for example, for ISO9000 and management development.

Looking slightly further ahead, the agency takes on additional activities and responsibilities, initially in the field of tourism, becoming a *de facto* regional development agency.

Falling leaves

Notwithstanding the ADE's excellent start, due to a misunderstanding between TACIS and KHF, TACIS funding is withdrawn. The agency does not yet have sufficient other funders and generates too little by way of fees. Other donor support withers away. Kiev ADE cannot provide enough support to keep the agency going, the western resident project manager leaves, local entrepreneurs cannot afford sufficient fees even to cover the reduced costs and the agency collapses.

Here are a few thoughts about the next 20 years or so – Shell have developed two scenarios reflecting possible global developments up to the year 2020 (see Herkströter, 1996).

Case study: Shell scenarios

'Just do it'

Their first scenario envisages a global trading system, driven by free trade, with almost unlimited competition. This allows for the fullest expression of individual creativity. Innovation is rapid and continuous. Technology is used to identify and to exploit opportunities. The societies that prosper are those that are individualist, entrepreneurial and fast moving.

'Da Wo'

Shell's second scenario takes its name from the Chinese expression for the place of the individual in the community. Countries and companies discover that success requires a committed investment in relationships. Trust – between individuals and enterprises and between enterprise and governments – is built up and sustained for competitive advantage. There is a shared belief that individual welfare is linked to the welfare of the whole. Government play an enabling role and there is a general acceptance of rights and responsibilities. The countries that prosper are those which are more cohesive and where social considerations are given more weight by business enterprises.

As Shell observe, these two scenarios are complementary. In Britain, Da Wo in particular can be seen in the voluntary sector, and in the increasingly high expectations of what business should do in and for the community.

A smaller business is not in any way able to influence which of these scenarios comes to pass. Indeed, nor is a large business. But there are considerable implications for businesses of all sizes. Think about the possible implications for your business. Perhaps businesses will have to do more, and to be seen to be doing more, in the community as the Royal Society for the encouragement of Arts, Manufactures and Commerce (RSA) suggests. Perhaps more effort will have to be made to develop and maintain effective networks. Perhaps more consideration will have to be given to public perceptions of businesses' ethics and values.

The Foresight Research Centre,[1] at the University of Durham, has been looking at the driving forces which will specifically impact on small and medium enterprises. They have looked ahead 10 years and have described three scenarios which may be of particular interest.

Case study: Foresight Research Centre scenarios

'Positive diversity'

In this scenario we can anticipate an economic environment in which people are confident about the future and social and business diversity are common. There will be a greater acceptance of risk and failure and more emphasis on skills and learning. One consequence would be an increase in the numbers of people running their own businesses, stimulated by new opportunities in information and communication technology and multimedia. There will be increased trade amongst smaller manufacturing businesses as well as for consultants and growth in personal services. The status in society of people who run their own business will increase. In short, running your own business is recognized and encouraged.

'Natural selection'

Society will be fragmented and fearful. Global corporations will dominate – both business and society. Small businesses' best hope will simply be survival. It is likely that more people will become self-employed, partially as a response to increasing unemployment and fewer employment opportunities. Smaller businesses will need to get – and remain – close to large firms. They will find the competition increasingly tough, as larger businesses increase their control over all links in the supply chain, dictating technical, business and ethical standards. Small businesses will feel powerless and disenfranchised.

'Opportunistic survival'

An ever increasing diversity of consumer demands will become the dominant force, to which businesses will respond by concentrating on market niches which, as a result, multiply quickly. Indeed, this niche thinking is replicated socially and in employment terms. Average firm size reduces, though more of their work is carried out under the control of larger firms, who control the global markets. The business environment is one which is extremely competitive but full of opportunities. Niches come and go so there is likely to be a high churn rate amongst smaller businesses. There is also likely to be a growing inter-dependence between small and large companies. Continuing training and development becomes more important.

Steps to developing scenarios

Step one: Identify focal issue or decision

Begin from within the business rather than from the wider environment. That is, begin with a specific decision or issue, then build out toward the environment. What will decision makers in your company be thinking hard about in the near future? What are the decisions that have to be made that will have a long-term influence on the fortunes of the company. In particular, aim to ensure a common understanding of the important features which influence your business.

Scenarios that are developed on the basis of differences in the macro-economy – high growth versus low growth, say – may not highlight issues that make a difference to a particular company. A graphic design business will be interested in whether customers will continue to use printed catalogues or will migrate to the Internet. A business selling ISDN modems will be interested in the increased use of electronic communications by large companies. A business selling roof windows will be interested both in the forecast of new housing starts and also in forecasts of people likely to engage in loft conversion. A person buying a home will want to think about interest rates and the housing market.

Begin with important decisions that have to be made 'Shall we invest in a proposed joint venture?' 'Shall we start to export?' 'Shall I start a new business?' 'Most of all, what is it that keeps me awake at night?' Define the scope and timescale for the scenario – ideally looking ahead at least 3–5 years.

Step two: Key forces in the local environment

This is where you begin to develop a model of how things work. Listing the key factors influencing the success or failure of the decision is the second step – facts about customers, suppliers, competitors, etc. What will decision makers want to know when making key choices? What will be seen as success or failure? What are the considerations that will shape those outcomes?

Step three: Driving forces and critical uncertainties

The third step involves listing the driving forces in the macro-environment that influence the key factors already identified. What are the PEST factors? What are the forces behind the micro-environmental forces identified in step two? Some of these forces are predetermined (say, demographics) and some are highly uncertain (say, public opinion). It is helpful to know what is inevitable and necessary and what is unpredictable and still a matter of speculation.

It can be useful to imagine oneself in the future saying, 'If only I had known that' inflation would fall, or that a new competitor would emerge from another country, or that regulations would change drastically.

This is the most research-intensive step in the process. In order to define the driving forces adequately research is usually required. Research may cover markets, new technology, political factors, economic forces, and so on, searching for the major trends and the trend breaks.

Step four: Rank by importance and uncertainty

Next comes the ranking of key factors and driving trends on the basis of two criteria: first, the degree of importance for the success of the decision identified in step one; second, the degree of uncertainty surrounding those factors and trends. The aim is to identify the two or three factors or trends that are most important and most uncertain.

Scenarios cannot differ over predetermined elements, say, the inevitable ageing of the baby boomers, because they are bound to be the same in all scenarios.

Step five: Selecting scenario themes

The results of this ranking exercise are, in effect, the axes along which the eventual scenarios will differ. Determining these axes is among the most important steps in the entire scenario-generating process. The goal is to end up with just two or three scenarios whose differences make a difference to decision makers. If the scenarios are to function as useful learning tools, the lessons they teach must be based on issues basic to the success of the focal decision. And those fundamental differences – or 'scenario drivers' – must be few in number in order to avoid a proliferation of different scenarios around every possible uncertainty.

Once the fundamental axes of crucial uncertainties have been identified, it is sometimes useful to present them as a spectrum (along one axis), or a matrix (with two axes), or a volume (with three axes) in which different scenarios can be identified and their details filled in.

The logic of a given scenario will be characterized by its location in the matrix of most significant scenario drivers. For example, if a graphic design business determines that pricing and use of electronic communications are the most important scenario drivers, there will be four basic scenario logics – because price can be high or low and use of electronic communications can be high or low.

The challenge is identifying the plot that best captures the dynamics of the situation and communicates the point effectively. For example, one scenario might be built around the logic of challenge and response: the challenge of foreign competition through increased use of electronic communications and closeness to the customer. Other plots might be based on winners and losers; evolution, revolution or cycles.

Pay attention to naming your scenarios. Names should succeed in capturing the scenario logics. If the names are vivid and memorable, the scenarios will have a much better chance of making their way into the decision making and decision implementing process across the company.

Step six: Fleshing out the scenarios

While the most important forces determine the logics that distinguish the scenarios, fleshing out the skeletal scenarios can be accomplished by returning to the lists of key factors and trends identified in steps two and three.

Each key factor and trend should be given some attention in each scenario. Sometimes it is immediately apparent which side of an uncertainty should be located in which scenario, sometimes not. If two scenarios differ over protectionist or non-protectionist policies, then it probably makes sense to put a higher inflation rate in the protectionist scenario and a lower inflation rate in the non-protectionist scenario. It is just such connections and mutual implications that scenarios should be designed to reveal.

Then weave the pieces together in the form of a narrative. How would the world get from here to there? What events might be necessary to make the end point of the scenario plausible?

Step seven: Implications

Once the scenarios have been developed in some detail, then it is time to return to the focal issue or decision identified in step one to rehearse the future. How does the decision look in each scenario? What vulnerabilities have been revealed? Is the decision or strategy robust across all scenarios, or does it look good in only one or two of the scenarios? If a decision looks good in only one of several scenarios, then it qualifies as a high-risk gamble – a bet-the-company strategy – especially if the company has little control over the likelihood of the required scenario coming to pass. How could that strategy be adapted to make it more robust if the desired scenario shows signs of not happening? How might your competitors react to each scenario? The results of your impact analysis may be helpful here.

Use the scenarios to help with contingency planning.

Step eight: Selection of leading indicators and signposts

It is important to know as soon as possible which of several scenarios is closest to the course of history as it actually unfolds. Sometimes the direction is obvious, especially with regard to factors like the health of the overall economy, but sometimes the leading indicators for a given scenario can be subtle. How, for example, should one calibrate the speed of economic restructuring from a smokestock economy towards an information-intensive economy?

Once the different scenarios have been fleshed out and their implications for the focal issue determined, then it's worth spending time and imagination on identifying a few indicators to monitor. If those indicators are selected carefully and imaginatively, the company will gain a jump on its competition in knowing what the future holds for a given industry and how that future is likely to affect strategies and decisions in the industry.[2]

Opportunities and threats

Once you have prepared your scenarios you will need to consider how your business will respond. What opportunities and threats are posed by each of the scenarios? How should you address each of those? How do you want to position your business in the external environment? What can you do now to achieve that? Define your responses dependent on the milestones. And then watch for the milestones.

Do try to prepare some scenarios – keep them basic if you like. Do not worry if you prepare scenarios that do not eventually come to pass; as you practise identifying driving forces, predetermined elements and critical uncertainties, watch how the future compares to your options. Then you will become more skilled at scenario planning.

The most difficult part in using scenarios is determining the critical uncertainties and then using them to help you decide how your business should respond. Once you have developed your scenarios and thought through the implications, you are in a position to build.

Build a map which defines the options open to the business (vision; unique selling point; competitive positioning; what business you are in; etc.). You can then define and prioritize the work needed in order to decide between those options; and, set up a mechanism to deliver.

Considering the implication of each of your scenarios for your business should enable you to add to the SWOT analysis developed in the previous chapter. What are the opportunities and threats? Having a thorough understanding will be a strength, but you will need to think more deeply about your own strengths and weaknesses to ensure you are not overwhelmed.

Conclusion

In this chapter, we have looked carefully at possible futures and have thought through the likely implications. You will need to make time to be foresightful and to construct scenarios – but it will be time well spent. Your competitors will certainly be thinking about the future, so do not give them any advantage. There is a considerable amount of information and intelligence around, as described in the previous chapter, so set up a system to capture it – and take time out occasionally to think about the future. Use the analysis to add to your understanding of opportunities and threats and to highlight further your strengths and weaknesses.

Rapid change makes it increasingly difficult to predict the future. Furthermore, yesterday's solutions are unlikely to work with tomorrow's problems. This uncertainty means that it is difficult for anyone to set out where they expect to be in 5 or 10 years' time. On the other hand, uncertainty and change bring opportunities to offer new products or new services, especially if you are one of the first to spot those opportunities. And those businesses which have a clear vision and clear sense of purpose will be the ones who can spot the opportunities which they can exploit to most advantage.

Remember the words of the American chessmaster, Emanuel Lasker, and apply them to your business: 'Victory in a game of chess belongs to him who sees a little further than his adversary'.

Notes

1 For further information, contact Foresight Research Centre, Durham University Business School, Mill Hill Lane, Durham, DH1 3LB, e-mail foresight@durham.ac.uk web site http://www.dur.ac.uk/foresight

2 Adapted from Peter Schwartz, *The Art of the Long View*, John Wiley and used with permission.

CHAPTER FOUR

Looking inwards

Strengths

If you are already in business, you may want to spend a little time thinking about the strengths of your business. Are they in the skills and competence of your staff? Are they in your product? Are they in your assets? Or your intellectual property? How sustainable are those strengths? Answering these questions may also highlight weaknesses. How do you defend yourself against the weaknesses? How do you build on your strengths?

Internal influences

In the last two chapters we have looked in detail at the market place and at the wider environment in which your business is working and we have also looked ahead, in an effort to determine trends and identify possible implications for both the market place and the environment. A business is subject to other influences – which arise from inside the business itself. These include the values and beliefs not only of the owners but also of the staff who work in the business which may of course be shaped by the values of the wider society, the culture of the business, the way in which the business is managed and the competence of the staff. If your customers are concerned about your values, it will be essential to be able to articulate them. But even without such pressure, you will almost certainly find it helpful to have an understanding of shared values in your business. In this chapter we will look inwards, concluding by completing the summary of strengths and weaknesses.

History

If you are already in business, and particularly if you have been in business for some time, it may help to start by looking at how you got to where you are today. Think, for a moment, about defining moments in the history of your business. Have those defining moments lead to changes in purpose, or in culture? It is interesting to note, for example, that many of the long lived companies cited in *The Living Company* (Geus, 1997) are now doing something different from what they did when they started – though they have all largely retained the same values framework. What has been critical to your success to date?

Values, style and behaviour

Values and beliefs are different in different societies and change over time. In one sense, they may be regarded as an external influence on a business because they provide an ethical framework in which any business has to operate. This is becoming very important. Consumers are concerned about values. Look at the success, for example, of Body Shop. And the dramatic growth, particularly in the USA, of ethical investing. Indeed, the Centre for Tomorrow's Company suggests that businesses should be more open and promote what they stand for and how they monitor their own behaviour. They believe that this will, in turn, make the public trust business more. Bribery and corruption are seen as unethical in the UK, for example, but there are other parts of the world where it is seen as normal business practice. Most people regard it as important to stay within the law – but then conclude that there are some laws which it is acceptable to break. How often do you speed, for example? Have you ever taken more than your duty free allowance through customs without declaring it? And once you've started, where do you stop? People in one of the more disadvantaged areas of Newcastle, for example, regard theft and shoplifting as acceptable, but generally frown on child abuse.

It has been said that rules are for the obedience of fools and the guidance of wise men – but if the rules are there to guide, rather than to cover every eventuality, there needs to be a value framework. This has to be a better approach than having too many rules and is particularly important in businesses, especially smaller businesses. If you are the owner manager then your own values and beliefs, and those of your staff will have an impact on what your business does and the way in which it operates.

Values may be quite general but will nevertheless be firmly held – importance of hard work, honesty, desire to continue learning, respect for the law, responsibility, respect for one another, dislike of corruption, fairness, thrift, desire to serve the community versus, perhaps, the importance of profit, for example. Values are closely linked to individuals' personal drivers. What drives you? A desire to achieve, ambition, doing everything to the best of one's ability, being creative and innovative, likely reward, etc.? Are you competitive and individualistic – or concerned about the environment and co-operative? Do you dominate or seek a partnership approach? Are you materialistic?

Personal values affect the way that we behave; and the way that an organization behaves depends on its staff's beliefs and behaviours. It is possible to alter our behaviour, so that we behave contrary to our values. But that creates a tension and we tend, in due course, to revert back to our natural behaviour. Widely shared values are likely to lead to harmony. The most successful organizations are those where the staff share similar values and moral principles since these guide individual and corporate behaviour, and where those values reinforce the organization's purpose. Shared values are likely to lead to mutual trust and to consistent decision making. If everyone in the business believes everyone will take the 'right' decision in a given set of circumstances, then there is less need for hierarchical control and more scope to encourage personal responsibility and initiative. This will probably result not only in a stronger focus on achieving the business's goals but also in a more motivated workforce.

The Institute for Global Ethics, based in the USA, argues the same. They point out that whilst rules and procedures may help to prevent bad decisions, they do not necessarily help to make good decisions. Nor can rules build openness, trust and credibility. Instead, they argue, leaders must demonstrate, through their own behaviour, the values which build trust. Appropriate ethical values, clearly articulated, will provide the best guidance for dealing with the complex ethical dilemmas that abound.

If, on the other hand, staff have very different values, there is likely to be dissonance, argument and ultimately failure. Imagine, for example, the problem of working in a business where the profit motive is paramount if you wish to serve the public; or wanting to be managed by a democratic, consultative manager but finding yourself with an autocratic boss.

When properly harnessed, shared values create 'a sense of purpose beyond making money that guides and inspires people throughout the organisation' (Collins and Porras, 1994). Increasingly, private sector companies are becoming more explicit about their corporate values, often attempting to encapsulate them into a statement of beliefs, even though this may lead to confusion about whether the values are really the shared values of the staff or are, in fact, the staff's view of what values are held important by the company. However they have been developed, a business's values should provide an essential and enduring set of general guiding principles. They are something to strive for in spite of changes to the environment. As hinted at earlier, such a statement might include the need to achieve, the desire to help others, the belief that an organization must behave ethically, the desire to develop one's own abilities and expertise, etc.

The company for which I mainly work articulates its philosophy as set out in the following case study.

Case study: Project North East

Project North East is a people-centred, non-profit organization which aims to be approachable, open, flexible and mutually supportive. It sees its target audience defined, neither by number of employees nor by turnover, but by people or organizations 'doing things for the first time'. PNE stresses the importance of being customer focused and of setting, and achieving, high standards. To do that effectively, it promotes a culture of continuing self-development, learning and teamwork.

PNE staff strive to respect and trust one another. The diversity of skills and experience at PNE is one of its strengths. All staff share a responsibility to develop new initiatives, to keep PNE at the forefront, and are rewarded by the opportunity to put those initiatives into practice.

Project North East aims to back up its words with actions. For example, it not only stresses the importance of continuing professional development but gives all staff 40 hours per annum to undertake training and provides everyone with a personal development budget.

Case study: British Telecom

British Telecom has published the following statement of their values:[1]

'We put our customers first
We are professional
We respect each other
We work as a team
We are committed to continuous improvement'

Stakeholders' perceptions of the business will depend on how they see the business behave. Do they see a helpful organization? A caring organization? A ruthless organization?

As mentioned above, some large businesses develop these statements to show how they relate to customers, as partly demonstrated by the BT statement above. This is fine, but belief in these values must really be shared by staff if the desired effect on behaviour is to be achieved. This relationship between values and behaviour is particularly important when organizations want to change their culture. For example, many businesses are currently encouraging their staff to think about quality and to build into their culture behaviours which reinforce the quality of their product or service.

Some people have difficulty in separating their personal values and those that they perceive that their employer finds desirable. You may prefer, therefore, to prepare a company 'philosophy' which encapsulates both of these. Nissan UK, for example, has a published statement which encapsulates the company's purpose as well as the way it hopes to achieve it:

Case study: Nissan

'Nissan's Sunderland plant aims to build profitably the highest quality car sold in Europe, to achieve the maximum possible customer satisfaction and thus ensure the prosperity of the company and its staff.

'To assist this we aim for mutual trust and co-operation between all people within the plant. We believe in teamworking wherein we encourage and value the contribution of all individuals who are working together towards a common objective and who continuously seek to improve every aspect of our business. We aim for flexibility in the sense of expanding the role of all staff to the maximum extent possible and we put quality consciousness as the key responsibility above all. We genuinely build in quality rather than inspect and rectify.

'These tough targets are assisted by the fact that we give common terms and conditions of employment to all our staff ...

'All this means that we believe that high calibre, well trained and motivated people are the key to our success.'[2]

Case study: Levi Strauss

Levi Strauss has a manifesto which highlights their mission, their aspirations and the type of leadership they believe is necessary to deliver their aspiration:[3]

'We all want a company that our people are proud of and committed to, where all employees have an opportunity to contribute, learn, grow and advance based on merit, not politics or background. We want our people to feel respected, treated fairly, listened to and involved. Above all, we want satisfaction from accomplishments and friendships, balanced personal and profes-sional lives, and to have fun in our endeavours.'

When employees join a business, there will inevitably need to be a compromise between what they believe and the values of the business. The objective, therefore, must be to minimize the difference between the two. This is more obvious when people join a political party or offer to do voluntary work – they seek like minded people with similar beliefs. But it is often ignored when people go to work! Christopher Bartlett and Sumantra Ghoshal (1994) believe that being clear about your beliefs and values will help organizations to 'attract and retain employees who identify with their values and become deeply committed to the organisation that embodies them'. They go on to suggest that individuals 'extract the most basic sense of purpose from the personal fulfilment they derive from being part of any organisation'. It is, therefore, essential that you, as you employ staff, rise to that challenge by creating 'an energising corporate purpose'.

The Co-operative Bank has identified seven stakeholders, or partner groups as they call them: customers, staff and their families, their shareholder (that is, their parent), their suppliers, their local communities, society at large and past and future generations. The bank has set out in some detail its core values. As might be expected, coming from the Co-operative Movement, they build on traditional co-operative values believing that businesses should have a purpose beyond profit. These underlying principles which provide guidelines for their business behaviour, are detailed in their mission statement.[4]

Case study: The Co-operative Bank

We, The Co-operative Bank Group, will continue to develop a successful and innovative financial institution by providing our customers with high quality financial and related services whilst promoting the underlying principles of co-operation which are:

- Quality and Excellence: To offer all our customers consistent high quality and good value services and strive for excellence in all that we do.

- Participation: To introduce and promote the concept of full participation by welcoming the views and concerns of our customers and by encouraging our staff to take an active role within the local community.

- Freedom of association: To be non-partisan in all social, political, racial and religious matters.

- Education and training: To act as a caring and responsible employer encouraging the development and training of all our staff and encouraging commitment and pride in each other and the Group.

- Co-operation: To develop a close affinity with organisations which promote fellowship between workers, customers, members and employers.

- Quality of life: To be a responsible member of society by promoting an environment where the needs of local communities can be met now and in the future.

- Retentions: To manage the business effectively and efficiently, attracting investment and maintaining sufficient surplus funds within the business to ensure the continued development of the Group.

- Integrity: To act at all time with honesty and integrity and within legislative and regulatory requirements.

They see interdependence, embracing both competition and co-operation, as essential to long-term success.

The Co-operative Bank's business performance continues to improve, perhaps confirming the RSA's assertion that businesses which take an inclusive approach, and which do not regard profit as the sole objective of business, are successful commercially as well as contributing to society.

Smaller businesses may well have difficulty emulating the Co-operative Bank's behaviour and are unlikely to share the Bank's view of its partners. Hopefully, however, their approach may give some food for thought. Certainly, businesses which have clear and shared values are likely to be businesses in which the staff are helped to achieve their own individual goals. In particular, they are likely to be the ones which enable every member of staff to achieve their potential.

Shell has a 'Statement of General Business Principles' which they give to all prospective employees and which sets out what they believe in and what they expect: values include honesty, integrity, respect for people, trust, openness, teamwork, professionalism and pride; expected behaviour includes upholding Shell's reputation, acting honestly and, at all times, doing what one thinks is right. Furthermore, Mark Moody-Stuart, Chairman of The Shell Transport & Trading Company, argues (Moody-Stuart, 1997) that profit alone is not the only motivation of business. Like individuals, companies have multiple roles and obligations and, when roles are contradictory, there can be dilemmas for managers. He stresses both the need to build long-term relationships – with customers, suppliers and all their stakeholders, and also the need to train and develop staff. Shell, being large, underpins all this with procedures designed to ensure staff understand the principles and act accordingly.

Case study: Shell

Shell companies recognize five areas of responsibility:

(a) To shareholders
To protect shareholders' investment, and provide an acceptable return.

(b) To customers
To win and maintain customers by developing and providing products and services which offer value in terms of price, quality, safety and environmental impact, which are supported by the requisite technological, environmental and commercial expertise.

(c) To employees
To respect the human rights of their employees, to provide their employees with good and safe conditions of work, and good and competitive terms and conditions of service, to promote the development and best use of human talent and equal opportunity employment, and to encourage the involvement of employees in the planning and direction of their work, and in the application of these principles within their company. It is recognised that commercial success depends on the full commitment of all employees.

(d) To those with whom they do business
To seek mutually beneficial relationships with contractors, suppliers and in joint ventures and to promote the application of these principles in so doing. The ability to promote these principles effectively will be an important factor in the decision to enter into or remain in such relationships.

(e) To society
To conduct business as responsible corporate members of society, to observe the laws of the countries in which they operate, to express support for fundamental human rights in line with the legitimate role of business and to give proper regard to health, safety and the environment consistent with their commitment to contribute to sustainable development.

These five areas of responsibility are seen as inseparable. Therefore it is the duty of management continuously to assess the priorities and discharge its responsibilities as best it can on the basis of that assessment.

Many small businesses may well be tempted to dismiss any thoughts of values and ethics as irrelevant. Certainly, a survey amongst Project North East clients suggests that, on the whole, other than wanting a sense of fair play all round, they feel that they cannot be too choosy. On the other hand, increasingly larger companies are devising their own ethical policies – and stating that they expect the same of their suppliers. B&Q,

for example, will only take hardwoods from renewable forests. Body Shop is well known for not testing its products on animals. Levi Strauss publishes an ethical policy in which it explains that it requires business partners to follow workplace standards and business practices consistent with its own policies. These include ethical standards, meeting legal requirements, environmental requirements, community involvement and employment standards.

John Collins and Jerry Porras (1994) believe that a business ideology is of over-riding importance: 'visionary companies display a powerful desire for progress that enables them to change and adapt without compromising their cherished core ideals'.

Values checklist

Here is a short list of areas which may be helpful in prompting a discussion about values:

- ambition;
- attitude to learn;
- equality of opportunity;
- honesty;
- impartiality;
- openness;
- ownership;

- personal responsibility;
- recognition for achievement;
- respect for others;
- sensitivity;
- teamwork;
- tolerance;
- trust.

Culture

Octo Industrial Design describes its culture thus: 'At Octo we have stacks of energy and boundless enthusiasm. We are an active and dedicated team who care, support each other and have fun'. This says a lot about the staff, but it also points towards how they expect to help their clients.

What is the culture in your business? It is likely to reflect the values of everyone who works in it, but it will mostly be influenced by you. Culture is really embodied in the phrase, 'the way we do things round here' . Often the way is taken for granted – the more often something is done in the same way, the more it becomes part of the culture and there can be dangers with this. People make assumptions, or do things the way they think it ought to be done, ultimately leading to confusion. Does your business have a culture of care, ambition, loyalty, trust, confidence, understanding, quality, self-discipline, continuous improvement, team-work, use of initiative and getting the best out of people? How do you manage the business? Do you simply tell people what to do, or do you seek participation and involvement? Do you delegate? How do you keep in touch with what is happening? How do you motivate people? Do you have awards or some form of recognition or celebration for important events? Remember though culture should be empowering not a straightjacket. As your business grows, there will be change, sometimes considerable and rapid change. Does the culture support change – or stifle it?

Ideally, the culture will not only tolerate but also encourage and stimulate debate. But there must be a process for taking decisions, and when the debate is over, and the decision taken, for better or for worse, the culture must accept the decision and move on.

As the business grows, and as a culture develops, you will inevitably get to the point at which you will need to recruit staff who fit the culture – since that is usually easier than changing the culture to fit new staff. I well remember one senior member of staff of the organization for which I work saying at a meeting of all the project managers that 'we had to change the culture to get the right staff' to which I suggested that an alternative view was to take more care to recruit staff so that they fitted the culture. My colleague was gone within a year! Culture is not imposed – it grows up as 'the way we do things round here', a sort of unwritten rule book. John Smith's, the brewery, aims to ensure it recruits people who will fit their culture explaining at interview that whilst they may not share John Smith's values when they start, they will have to behave in accordance with them. Ben & Jerry's, a US ice cream manufacturer with a reputation for its social conscience screens all potential staff to ensure that they share the founders' values. This does not mean, however, that all your staff have to be clones. Having similar values still leaves plenty of scope for diversity and this should be encouraged in order to gain the creative spark that comes from people sharing ideas. But the culture, unlike values, can be changed, if there is enough of a will, and sometimes has to be in order for the business to grow.

The first need is to understand the existing culture; the second is to know what sort of culture is desired. You may wish, for example, to instil an achievement oriented culture, where the focus is on success rather than simply on effort. This will need to be underpinned by a manage-ment structure which encourages learning and coaching in order to achieve agreed objectives (supporting the 'do' part of the Plan-Do-Check-Act cycle) and by appropriate means of measuring performance (supporting the 'check' part) and giving feedback. You may encourage a culture where people can take initiatives themselves, where they can take responsibility for decisions, where they can take risks, most of all where they know the boundaries.

Case study: John Lewis Partnership

The John Lewis Partnership was founded, in its current form, in 1929 by the son of John Lewis who had started his business many years earlier, in the belief that there was a way of doing business which was better and fairer and from which everyone could benefit. John Lewis already believed in offering service to customers – passing on cost advantages, immortalized in their credo 'never knowingly undersold'. The company ceased being a sole proprietorship and became a partnership trust, with all the staff becoming partners. It set out a written constitution, in terms strikingly similar to the principles of Tomorrow's Company. Like any other business, John Lewis Partnership is looking for financial rewards but it also recognizes it has responsibilities to customer, suppliers, staff and the community at large.

The company likes to think of its partners not as 'mercenaries', simply selling their labour to the highest bidder with no real interest in the outcome, but as 'citizens' who are loyal to the business, who share in its success and, importantly, who have a right to be heard.

This attitude pervades the company's culture. The weekly partners' newsletter, for example, encourages letters of complaint or suggestion for improvements. The management style is one of talk, discuss, agree – though this does not mean that they stand around in huddles over every decision. Clearly, if they are to compete with the best retailers (and that means some of the most efficient commercial operators in the country) then they have to match their standards of management. So all management decisions are open to scrutiny and subsequent accountability. Autocratic managers do not fit! The company aims to develop good relationships with their suppliers, noting that in engineering terms friction is the enemy of efficiency and that the same is true in business.

Arguably it is an organization's management style that has the biggest impact on culture, on the way the organization relates to staff and, consequently, on the way it relates to customers and other stakeholders. It is perhaps, therefore, worth looking at management styles in a little more detail.

Management styles

All managers develop their own style of management – but the culture of the organization can also have a major impact on the management style adopted (whether explicitly or implicitly) by the organization.

Four clear cultures have been identified – club, role, task and existential. Charles Handy (1985) has given them all names after Greek gods – Zeus, Apollo, Athena and Dionysus.

The club culture resembles a spider's web. This culture is typically found in small, family owned businesses where the owner is at the centre. Family or other managers have direct lines of communication. What the owner says, goes. Everyone else either seeks agreement or simply second guesses. As a result, everyone tends to think in the same sort of way. As Handy says, they work 'on empathetic initiative with personal contact rather than formal liaison'.

The role culture is one familiar to most people. Roles, or duties, are fixed. Management tends to be very hierarchical. Power lies at the top. The tasks of the organization are divided giving organizational work flows with prescribed roles and comprehensive roles and procedures. Role cultures are efficient when work is predictable but they do not cope well with change.

The task culture is more suited to people working in teams where the key requirement is to solve problems through the allocation of appropriate resources. This culture recognizes is one where creativity is regarded as important; it is the ability to be creative that confers influence. Leadership is not usually an issue since the teams are committed to solving the problems – and to helping each other when they run into difficulties.

The last culture, the existential culture, is typically seen in universities and the NHS. This culture assumes that we are in charge of our own destinies. In the other three cultures, the individual is there to assist the organization achieve its purpose. In this culture, the individuals see the role of the organization as simply being to help them achieve their purposes. People in this culture do not recognize a boss.

Clarity about the sort of management style you would like to foster, makes it easier to think about the sort of organizational structure you need to implement your strategy.

FIGURE 4.1 Management styles

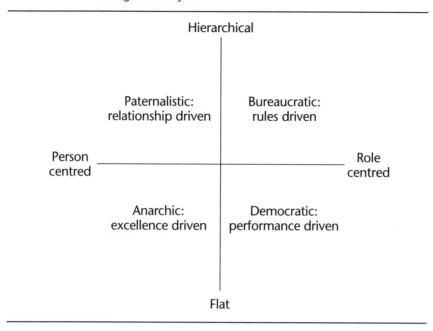

Most businesses typically start with the club culture – with the entrepreneur at the middle. They know what they want. They don't always communicate it very well, but they do expect their staff to get it right! As the business grows, they have to start relinquishing control, though some entrepreneurs take a conscious decision not to grow too much so as not to lose that control. Entrepreneurs have to learn to delegate – not always easy – and to delegate authority along with responsibility. Many businesses then adopt the hierarchical, role style of management. As businesses are increasingly knowledge based, however, many people prefer the freedom that comes with a less hierarchical, more task based style of management. It is not possible to be prescriptive – you have to develop the one that works for you – always remembering that the organization's management style will become an important part of the culture.

In the task oriented culture, it is likely that staff will all find themselves working in teams. They might do so in the other cultures as well but, as stated earlier, this culture is particularly appropriate for teamworking. As more businesses recognize the importance of teamwork, in which staff draw from and work with others, it makes sense to think about how to get the best out of teams. This is something that we will return to in the last chapter.

Sensitivity and tolerance

Arie de Geus (1997), who was for several years in charge of Shell's scenario planning team, asserts that 'companies die because their managers focus on the economic activity of producing goods and service and they forget that their organization's true nature is that of a community of humans'. He is not suggesting for one moment that managers should lose sight of the economic purpose of their business but rather stressing that getting the human relationships right will almost certainly result in getting the business's external relationships right which, in turn, will enable it to achieve its economic purpose.

De Geus has identified four characteristics of long lived companies, all of which are cultural:

- Businesses which are sensitive to the environment in which they operate develop the abilities to learn and adapt.

- Businesses which are cohesive develop a strong persona – the staff feel part of the business.

- Businesses which are tolerant are able to build strong and constructive relationships with stakeholders. These include the staff but also include all those organizations outside the business with which it deals. Tolerance derives from the shared values. Some companies take this a long way. 3M, for example, creates space for its staff to encourage creativity and innovation.

- Businesses which are financially conservative will stay in control of their growth and evolution. This doesn't stop them taking risks, but may stop them being too indebted, preferring to grow organically, or encouraging them only to take risks with their own money.

Knowledge, skills, abilities

Having shared values will undoubtedly help to ensure that your staff all pull in the same direction. But you also need to ensure that they have the competences required to do their work efficiently and effectively. To complete your analysis of strengths and weaknesses, therefore, you need to look at the business's core competences (the *sine qua non* which gives your business its competitive advantage) and at your staff's individual skills and knowledge.

Like so much else, this is a regular and continuing requirement. It can be determined through job analysis – What is expected of staff? What is the purpose of their job? What are their targets and objectives? What are their duties and responsibilities? What is the required level of knowledge? What is the required skill level? What are the required abilities? It may be helpful to think about how jobs may develop and what will be required of staff in new or different or extended roles.

We will return in Chapter Seven to consider how to develop staff. What is important at this stage is to consider the strengths and weaknesses primarily of the business as a whole. What are the business's strengths? Are there strengths that are not being exploited? Perhaps of more immediate importance, what are the weaknesses or gaps? You may already have a shrewd idea of the business's strengths and weaknesses. If not, you may want to do more to measure the gap.

The process of measuring the gap between the requirements of the job and actual job performance is best conducted logically and with a generous helping of common sense. You will need to consider the job analysis and to have agreed standards of performance before you start. This will tell you what it is that is required. You are now ready to assess the current position which may be done in a number of ways, including:

- personal interviews;

- questionnaires;

- observations;

- assessments;

- quality control;

- monitoring:
  - staff conflict,
  - complaints from staff/customers,
  - absenteeism,
  - staff turnover/exit interviews,
  - accident reports.

You can use the results of your analysis to add to your SWOT matrix.

Resources

In his book *Management: Tasks, Responsibilities, Practices*, Drucker (1974) reminds us that all economic activity requires three kinds of resources:

natural or physical resources, human resources and financial resources. An organization must be able to attract all three and put them to productive use. Johnson and Scholes (1993) add one more: intangible resources. This might include, for example, the value of a brand name or goodwill.

Research by Barings Venture Partners amongst those businesses in which it has invested suggests that product development, strategic positioning and marketing are all important – but that real success depends on the way they manage their resources of people, information and money (Onians, 1995).

Resource management sounds as though it should be easy – but in reality it can be hard. The first step is to identify the specific activities required to implement your chosen strategy – we will look at this in more detail in Chapter Six. Then you need to consider the specific resource requirements for each stage. Are those resources already available within the business? Do you need to attract additional resources – extra money, perhaps, or people with specialist skills?

If you pursue a cost leadership strategy, then you need to be extremely efficient at every stage in the process of getting your product or service into the hands of your customers. Not only does the manufacturing process need to be efficient and effective – round the clock working, for example, to maximize machine usage – but marketing costs, distribution costs and overhead costs all need to be controlled very tightly. You will be particularly looking for innovations in the processes that lead to cost savings.

If you choose to pursue a strategy of differentiation, then you have a different set of problems. Quality in the end product will require quality in materials and in all the processes that lead to the final product. Marketing may require more effort to position yourself more appropriately in the market place. Innovation is more likely to be in the development of the product. Think about the resources available in your business – if you like, split them into the categories of money, people and physical. If you do not have required resources how easy – or difficult – will it be to attract those resources? Add the results of your thinking to your SWOT matrix.

Conclusion

Since strategy aims to match competence and resource to the environment, you need to have a thorough understanding of your competences and resources in order to develop a workable strategy.

In this chapter we have taken a thorough look inwards at the business. You have completed the process of looking at opportunities and threats and of considering strengths and weaknesses. In particular, you have thought about how your values and culture both provide a foundation for and reinforce the activities of your business. You have thought about staff skills and gaps. You have considered the availability of resources and your ability to attract further resources. We can now go on to think about strategy.

Notes

1 Taken from an internal BT document.
2 Taken from a 1994 company profile for Nissan Motor Manufacturing (UK) Ltd.
3 From an internal Levi Strauss document.
4 Taken from a Co-operative Bank Plc mission statement.

CHAPTER FIVE

Defining a direction

Adding value

Whatever business you are in, you are aiming to sell a product or service to a customer. Customers buy benefits – if the features of your product or service do not provide the benefits sought by the customer, they will not buy. So in order to provide those benefits you will be adding value. For example, you manufacture windows. You take raw materials – in the form of timber and glass – and turn these materials into windows, adding considerable value in the process. Or you are an industrial designer – you take a concept from a customer, or maybe even assist the customer to develop the concept, and then turn that concept into a finished design.

Customers, though they may not put it in quite these words, will make buying decisions based on their perception of the balance between added value (along the entire supply chain) and price.

What customers buy and consider to be of value, then, will determine what the business is, what it produces and whether it will prosper. You, as an owner manager, will of course be aiming to position your product or service in such a way as to convince the customer that it really does offer the benefits that they are after. In other words, businesses should be market driven. You will recall that Peter Drucker (1968) argues that the two basic functions of a business are marketing and innovation so these are the key areas where you should aim for competitive advantage. Businesses which are market driven respond to the needs of their customers, whereas businesses which are product driven start with a product and then try to persuade customers to buy it. It is perhaps worth noting, however, that customers cannot always articulate the benefits they would like – as Sony demonstrated with their Walkman, or as thousands of children demonstrated at the end of the 1990s with the infernal Tamagotchi.

Purpose : *What the Business Does :*

Andrew Campbell, a founding director of the Ashridge Strategic Management Centre, (Campbell *et al.*, 1990) argues that businesses need to define four key elements: purpose, values, standards and behaviours, and strategy. In his words 'strategy will define the business that the company is going to compete in, the position that the company plans to hold in that business and the distinctive competence or competitive advantage that the company has or plans to create'.

Case study: Agromasina

Agromasina is located in Kishinev in Moldova. It manufactured agricultural equipment, concentrating on heavy duty trailers. In the old days of Soviet central planning it simply produced what it was told to produce. It never had to worry about marketing or the cost of capital. It is totally vertically integrated making everything, right down to the nuts and bolts, that comprise a complete trailer. With the collapse of communism and central planning, their market has completely collapsed and sales have all but disappeared. When I asked them what they did, they kept repeating, like a mantra, that they made specialist agricultural machinery. But what I saw, when I looked round, was an old fashioned mechanical engineering machine shop. They had equipment, and skills, in the basic cutting, pressing, stamping, forming, grinding, polishing and heat treating of iron and steel. They could actually turn their hand to making anything that requires those skills – opening up new customers and new markets.

Think further for a moment about your purpose. What business are you in? It may not be as obvious, at first sight, as you think it is. What is the business of Ronson lighters? Who is their biggest competitor? Matches perhaps? In reality, they are in the gift business. Look at the way they advertise – and when: buy a lighter for your partner this Christmas. So their major competitor is probably the Parker Pen company. MacConnect, a small business started in Newcastle, sold high speed computer modems for use with ISDN telephone lines. These are particularly attractive to design houses and their customers who often pass designs, say for an annual report, backwards and forwards as many as 40 times. The business struggled when it thought it was selling a high technology computer peripheral. Then it realized that its main competitor was motorcycle couriers and the business started to take off.

Most businesses, however, want more focus than simply creating customers and making a profit. They do something more specific – like making windows or being an industrial designer. Better still, they do something very specific – like making windows for roofs or offering design services in electrical white goods. Many businesses write down what they do in a mission statement. At its simplest, a mission statement is a statement of purpose that guides the activities of a business. It is what 'you do'. Defining a purpose is a pre-requisite for effective planning. Ideally, it should be easily understood by all the stakeholders that is, the owners, the customers, the staff and anyone else with a stake in the business.

The purpose statement should be the over-riding factor in guiding a business organization. Ideally, it should not only define the business but also its customers and differentiate it from its competitors. Some businesses have very long mission statements which set out all the organization's objectives. I believe, however, that a short purpose is more likely to excite and inspire the stakeholders and is more likely to be remembered by the staff.

One small business, Blooming Marvellous, defines its purpose by saying: 'We design, make and market clothes for the fashion conscious mother-to-be'. This states exactly what they do and exactly who they perceive as their customers. Octo Industrial Design says 'Octo's purpose is to produce consistently successful design solutions for clients who aspire to high quality design'. Levi Strauss, though rather larger, also have a simple statement: 'The mission of Levi Strauss & Co is to sustain profitable and successful commercial success by marketing jeans and selected casual apparel under the Levi's brand'. Apple Computer inject a core belief into their purpose: 'Our goal has always been to create the world's friendliest, most understandable computers – computers that empower the individual'. Giveway Internet, a small business based in Newcastle, simply say their purpose is 'To sell internet network software to Mac users'.

Case study: The Solution Design Consultants Ltd

This graphic design business has defined its purpose by stating 'The Solution design and produce marketing materials for companies who see their image as a priority for success.'

The business has set out a number of challenging goals in terms of how they see the business expanding, how they see the business taking an international outlook and how they see their work developing. They are keen specifically to work with businesses who share their values.

It is, however, their purpose statement which defines their target customers. As you might guess they expect to offer a premium product to people who are not overly concerned with price. They are, therefore, in a position to define their objectives accordingly.

Non-profit and voluntary organizations are often surprisingly good at articulating their purpose, usually because of a reliance, at least in part, on donor aid and a need, therefore, to express what they do cogently and concisely.

Case study: The Valley Trust, Republic of South Africa

'The mission of the Valley Trust is to offer quality education and training with associated resources in fields relating to comprehensive primary health care and sustainable development, to strengthen the capacity of individuals and communities to improve their quality of life.'

Increasingly, businesses are focusing on their core competences – these are the things that they do, or think they can do, better than anyone else. A natural consequence of this is the decision to sub-contract, or outsource, everything else. The Burton Group, mentioned earlier, used to manufacture clothes, but now concentrates on design and marketing and sub-contracts all of its manufacturing requirements. Nike does the same. Defining core competence is not always straightforward. The electricity distribution companies or the water companies may argue, for example, that their strengths are in billing of continuously delivered products – having large databases, and mechanisms for measuring consumption. It's then an easy jump for Northern Electric, for example, to justify its decision to sell gas. It doesn't actually distribute gas. It simply arranges bulk supply contracts, arranges distribution contracts, reads the meters and sends the bills. Similarly, Metro Radio sees itself, not in the radio business, but in the 'commodity business' – selling advertising opportunities.

Designers with innovative ideas for new products may decide to manufacture those products, or they may decide to license their ideas to a manufacturer and stick to doing what they do best – designing innovative products.

Some people will argue that having a narrowly focused purpose statement will constrain the business. On the one hand, for some businesses, this may be no bad thing. It can be very easy to flit from one idea to another, like a hawker selling whatever can be acquired cheaply. A carefully worded purpose will at least encourage entrepreneurs to ask the question whether they should be doing something completely different. On the other hand, the purpose is not supposed to be a straightjacket. If opportunities really do present themselves, then they should be seized. But do first consider whether the advantages of distracting yourself from your defined purpose will be worth more than the effective cost of the disadvantages. It is true that some people have been extremely successful in jumping – like Bill Gross for example (*The Economist*, 1997).

Bill Gross has started 24 companies in a year, now worth more than $220m. He, and his companies, churn out ideas for new businesses, many of which are in communication and software. Arguably, though, Bill Gross's purpose is simply to dream up new business ideas, develop companies to exploit them and then to hive them off.

If you have difficulty describing your purpose succinctly, try stepping into the shoes of your customers for a moment. What do they see? What benefits do they gain from buying your product or service? Who are they?

Coca-Cola, for example, promises 'refreshment'. All its marketing is geared to that end and it refuses to take its eye off the ball. It continues to outsell Pepsi by a huge margin, even though Pepsi usually wins in blind tastings. But while Pepsi has dabbled in other areas, Coke has stuck solely with delivering against its promise.

Challenging goals

Where do you want to be in five years' time? Reading a book on the veranda of your house in Spain perhaps? Running a business competing in international markets allowing you to travel the world? Owning the latest BMW? Perhaps entering politics like Geoffrey Robinson or Archie Norman! So you do have a vision – perhaps with both business and personal goals. Perhaps you're reading this because, although you currently work for someone else, you aim to start your own business.

Purpose expresses what the business does, but it is vision which drives the business forward. It is vision which sets a direction for the business. Vision is about having challenging, but achievable, goals with defined time scales. You may choose to pull these goals together into a single vision statement. Or you may prefer just to have two or three or four really challenging goals, with timescales. John Collins and Gerry Porras (1994) argue that the businesses which last are those that have 'big hairy audacious goals'. Indeed, for smaller businesses I think this makes considerable sense. It can take a long time to define a vision statement that makes sense and inspires and drives – whereas the right goal or goals are usually simpler to articulate and can be far more inspirational – like John Kennedy's goal to put a man on the moon before the end of the decade. This will help, in the words of Sumantra Ghoshal (1996), to 'create a climate of ambition'.

Goals can be about entering new markets, or bringing new products to market, or increasing market share.

Case study: British Biotech plc

When J D Searle was taken over, and later closed by Monsanto, the then Director of Research, Dr Keith McCullagh and ten colleagues decided to start their own biotechnology business. They had a simple, but challenging goal: 'to build an international pharmaceutical company'. Since their establishment in 1986, they have forged links with universities at Oxford, Cambridge, Edinburgh, around continental Europe and in the USA. They have raised over £342m in equity capital – though they have still not, quite, brought their first product to market. Yet, they say, raising finance has not been difficult because it has always been properly planned and because they have been able to demonstrate expected future returns to potential investors.

Case study: Hydro Technologies Ltd

Hydro Technologies aims, quite simply, to be a world class supplier of water jet cutting profiles, providing water jet cutting technology to at least half the countries of the world.

In developing goals, think outside what you currently do in order to imagine a future in which your business is important. Earlier, we talked about the importance of benchmarking. Benchmarking is important in order to help you keep up with, or aspire to keep up with, the best. But it doesn't help you become the best. You may need to do something extra to leapfrog your competitors – with your product or with your service. Simply asking customers or potential customers about their needs, both now and in the future, may not be enough to be innovative.

Gary Hamel and C. K. Prahalad (1994) noted from their research that some large company management teams 'were capable of imagining products, services and entire industries that did not yet exist and then giving them birth. These managers seemed to spend less time worrying about how to position the firm in existing competitive space and more time creating fundamentally new competitive space.' Sadly, most small businesses will have difficulty changing the environment – though if you can spot how to do it you will be on to a winner. Gary Hamel suggests that strategy can mean deciding what you would like the future market to look like – and then stretch your business's skills in order to take advantage of that market.

Do not make the process too complicated. You do need to have some idea of the environment in which you will operate; whilst you want the goals to be challenging, they also need to look as though they are achievable. Most small organizations are more likely to have to react to the environment rather than being able to influence it. Similarly, the consequences of getting it wrong will be different for a small organization compared, say, to Shell's decision whether to invest billions of pounds on a new North Sea gas platform. If a business's goals reflect its shared values then this will reinforce the likelihood of achieving the goals.

I sometimes find businesses which have difficulty articulating a vision. I have found the following role play enormously helpful. Try it now:

Imagine that the date is five years in the future. You are sitting down to write the Chairman's introduction to your annual report. What were the key achievements last year? Put those in the context of achievements over the last three years. Set out your objectives for the next year.

With luck that will help to imagine some visionary goals. Now rewrite the goals as something to be achieved in the future.

Inevitably smaller businesses are concerned with the here and now and the short-term future. Yes – of course, that's important. But if you really want to drive the business forward in a chosen direction, rather than drifting, you need to think ahead, in order to put in place the strategies to make it happen.

Strategies

Once you have defined your purpose and goals, then you can begin to think about the required action to ensure that you achieve your goals. The starting point for this is to brainstorm all possible options. You will then need to evaluate the options and, finally, choose one. This may seem obvious, but every option will have resource implications. Options may be affected or constrained by the organization's long-term direction, and by the values and expectations of its stakeholders. Options are likely to have implications for the organization's existing operational objectives. Strategy, then, builds on a business's long-term direction, matching available resources to the needs of the market place, in order to meet stakeholder expectations.

Michael Porter (1980) suggests that positioning in the market place is all important and, further, that the key to successful positioning is the right choice of what he calls generic strategies.

The way you choose to position your product will depend on how you plan to differentiate yourself from your competitors and your chosen target customers. It will be reflected in the way that you promote it and in the businesses that you perceive as competitors. It will also affect the way you see external factors and, in particular, opportunities and threats. It may affect the availability of resources. It will certainly affect the way that the business is perceived by its stakeholders including customers, suppliers and the community in which the business operates. All these, in turn, will affect your strategic objectives.

'Positioning' describes how you want customers to think of your product or service relative to those of competitors. Take as an example the difference between mid-range cars sold by Ford and BMW. In most respects both models of car are similar. Their function is identical – they are both designed to be a mode of personal transport. What makes them different is the pricing structure, styling and, perhaps most importantly, their respective perceived images. Ford want people to think of their mid-range products as affordable cars for the mass of average people, whereas BMW want people to think of their cars as the 'sensible' choice for discerning buyers amongst those who are 'successful'. What each company has done is choose a positioning for the product defined by the target customer group and the means by which the product is differentiated from others.

Once you have a feel for your target market and what it is that sets your product or service apart, you can consider which generic strategy you intend to adopt.

Businesses face the choice of going for a high volume mass market or a specific market segment or niche. In terms of product strategy, there are two primary choices – cost/price advantage usually referred to as cost leadership, or differentiation.

The combination of these choices leads to four possible positioning strategies, two of which (cost focus and differentiation focus) are very similar because both rely on inherent differences in the target sector (Porter, 1980).

In adopting a cost leadership approach a firm aims for high volume competing on price. The intention is to attain market leadership by undercutting all competitors – albeit marginally. That is not to suggest that the product is inferior. To ensure that customers will buy the product it must be of acceptable quality – either close to or as good as those of its competitors.

Successful use of this strategy depends on achieving, and maintaining, a significant cost advantage. The strategy of cost leadership is one that is commonly adopted, though rarely fully achieved. After all, it is difficult to make a reasonable profit unless you have a high volume of sales.

A strategy of differentiation is based on identifying a unique benefit that is highly valued by a substantial proportion of the target market. In this case, businesses differentiate themselves by offering a product which is different, usually by providing greater benefit, and are therefore able to set their prices higher. Häagen-Dazs and Ben & Jerry's have both pursued a strategy of differentiation for their ice cream – in the process creating a market for so-called super premium ice cream, now worth $261m per year in the USA alone, of which Ben & Jerry's has a 39 per cent market share.

FIGURE 5.1   Generic strategies

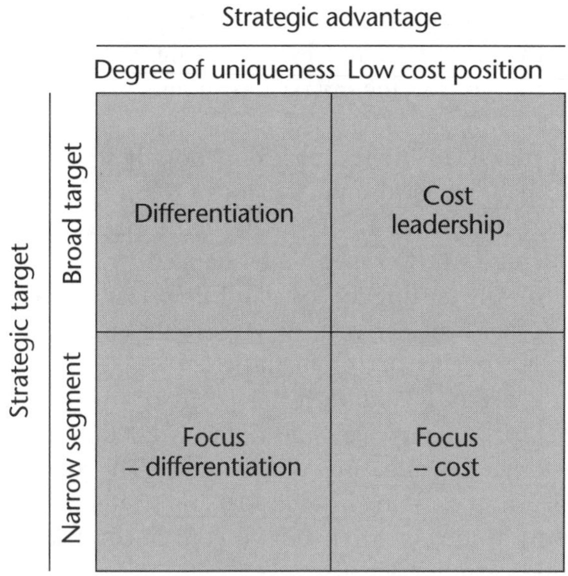

Strategic advantage

Degree of uniqueness   Low cost position

	Broad target	Differentiation	Cost leadership
Strategic target	Narrow segment	Focus – differentiation	Focus – cost

Source: Adapted from Porter, 1980

Both use ingredients of the highest quality, and with a commitment to luxury. Ben & Jerry's have gone further – being unconventional and stressing their support for worthy causes. Not everyone buys, or can afford to buy, premium priced, differentiated products – so the positioning will, to a certain extent, define the required marketing mix.

Some businesses, however, choose to focus on a particular niche market, product or service specifically adapted to suit the needs of the chosen niche. The difference between this approach and the mainstream differentiation strategy is that it relies on an inherent difference in customer preferences, attitudes and behaviour in the selected segment compared to the market overall. An example would be the TV market where, outside of the volume sectors of the market, some manufacturers have opted to serve a smaller segment such as the portable sector, or a specialist niche such as the big-screen units used in conference rooms. Here the customer requirements are quite different and cannot be met by minor adaptations of mainstream products.

Businesses which aim for a focused approach, however, are still likely to meet some competition and so need to decide whether, even within narrow target segments, to pursue cost leadership or differentiation.

Look, for example, at the market for personal computers. Many manufacturers attempted to emulate the IBM PC. Two stood out, offering a premium product at a premium price: Compaq and Apple. Apple further differentiated themselves by not even offering a compatible machine, instead focusing on specific market segments, such as educational markets.

Compaq makes an interesting case study. It started only in 1982 and, by 1988, had achieved annual sales of $2bn selling high quality, premium priced computers. In 1991 sales fell 9 per cent and net profit dropped by 71 per cent. Compaq then changed strategy to one of cost leadership, ruthlessly cutting its costs and its prices. Compaq price cuts now average 30 per cent per year. As you would expect, its gross profit margin has fallen but its net profit has risen. For 1997, sales were up, again, reaching nearly $25bn with net profit of over $2bn. Compaq's biggest competitors are now Dell and Gateway 2000, both of whom sell direct to customers eliminating dealer costs. The danger, for small businesses at least, in pursuing a cost leadership strategy is that customers tend to stay only as long as you maintain your price advantage. It is very difficult to build customer loyalty.

Choosing your positioning

Once you've looked widely outside the business – assessing the market place and wider environment – and at your own strengths, you will be able to look at what Porter regards as critical success factors: the attractiveness of a particular industry defined by the scope for long-term profitability and your competitive position within the industry. Both, of course, change constantly.

Market segmentation will help you to define your customers fairly accurately. How will they perceive your product or service? Will it be a high quality, high price, premium product or a low cost, low price, commodity product?

Many markets can have different companies each adopting one of the strategies and successfully coexisting. It is very rare for more than one or two businesses to succeed with a cost leadership strategy and, unless a market is particularly large, the same often applies for the high volume differentiation strategy. However, many markets contain small specialist sectors that are of little interest to the larger companies and so offer good opportunities to adopt a strategy of focus. This is one of the reasons why, in many cases though by no means all, the focus strategy proves to be the most appropriate for a smaller firm competing in markets where the high volume ground is already dominated by large businesses.

When choosing which of the generic strategies is most appropriate for your market you will need to consider the existing competitor situation: are they many or few? What strategies have they already adopted (if any)? Do you have a notable advantage over existing players? You will also need to apply the results of your research into customer attitudes and behaviour. Are there notable differences which have created obvious niches? Are there indications that it might be possible to create a new niche? Are there any identifiable requirements that are not currently being met which can thus be used as differentiation factors? Of course, markets are dynamic and subject to constant change. As you deliberate on the positioning you feel will be most appropriate, remember to look at the market trends as well as the current situation.

Gary Hamel and C. K. Prahalad (1994) point out that strategy has to be about more than simply positioning. Otherwise, businesses are in danger of forever playing catch-up with more foresighted competitors. In other words, positioning should reinforce the overall strategic approach, not be the sole determinant of it.

Marks & Spencer aim to sell high quality merchandise that offers good value for money. The big supermarkets, like Tesco and Sainsbury, take a similar approach. Cut price supermarkets, like Aldi, aim for cost leadership, which is achieved through being more like a warehouse than a supermarket, and through a greater reliance on own brand or 'down market' products.

First Direct opened up a whole new banking market, and kept their costs right down, by offering a telephone banking service all round the clock. They provide everything you get from any other bank – except a branch network!

Yeoman Pressings offer low prices initially to win customers, but then retain customers by providing a good service characterized by high quality standards and always meeting delivery deadlines. Giveway Internet differentiates itself by offering a specialized product to a narrow target audience. Hydro Technologies offers a good quality product to a niche market.

Increasingly, larger companies are recognizing the power of brands. A widespread desire by customers to own a particular brand results in higher premiums on the price. Witness, for example, Intel's remarkable success with its 'Intel Inside' campaign. Whilst Intel is only selling to computer manufacturers it has convinced customers of computers that they should only buy if they really do have Intel inside.

Smaller companies, too, can promote their brands though will not have the same marketing budget. You should be aiming for customer loyalty, repeat business and word of mouth recommendations to other potential customers.

You will also need to consider how you might defend your position. Can you manufacture on a large enough scale to erect a sizeable barrier to entry to potential competitors? Can you form a partnership with your key supplier to stop competitors using the same raw materials? Possibly best of all, is your business based on proprietary technology or intellectual property?

Once you have chosen your positioning, you can then think about the marketing mix – the 4Ps of product, price, promotion and place – in order to achieve sales of your product or service.

FIGURE 5.2   Marketing strategy

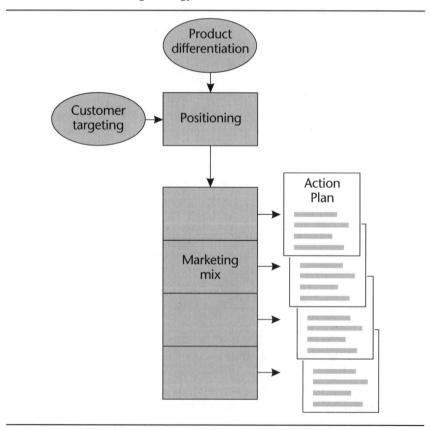

Product: What are your customers looking for?

It is important to satisfy the needs of your customers. When asked what his business did, Charles Revson, replied: 'In the factory, we make cosmetics; in the store we sell hope'. In other words, businesses sell *features,* but people buy *benefits* . This is true of every product or service. Eddie Jordan, proprietor of the Jordon Formula One Grand Prix team, says 'My job is selling a dream. I make racing cars and sell space on them, along with a platform for a marketing and hospitality package' (*Sunday Times*, 1997). He is offering space to advertisers trying to communicate an aspirational message – smoke Benson & Hedges and be like me.

Features are what a product has or is, for example size, colour, attachments, etc. Benefits are what the product does for the customer (Table 5.1).

It is important to remember that the seller pays for the features and that the customer buys the benefits. So successful marketing of a product involves communicating both features and benefits. Furthermore, those benefits must be worth more to the customer than the features cost you to deliver.

Maslow, the eminent American psychologist, suggested (Maslow, 1954) that 'all consumers are goal seekers who gratify their needs by purchase and consumption'. He classified consumer needs in a five stage pyramid known as the Hierarchy of Needs. The first and largest need was physiological (hunger and thirst), followed by safety, self-esteem and, at the top of the pyramid, self-realization.

Every product or service is bought to satisfy one or more of these needs. So, for example, as people's hunger and thirst needs are satisfied, they move up the hierarchy, to satisfy other needs.

Where are your customers on the needs' hierarchy and how can your product or service help them to achieve their goals? What do

TABLE 5.1 Features vs. benefits

Feature	*Benefit*
Leather seats	Comfort
Anti-lock brakes	Safety
Central locking	Security
1400cc lean burn engine	Economy
Catalytic converter	Environmentally friendly
Convertible	Style

customers think about the kind of product or services being offered? What are their likes and dislikes? What attributes are important to them? What features or promises would be most likely to make them use your product or service?

Understanding your market can also ensure that you are alive to changes in say, technology or customer preferences. Conversely, if you do not understand what you are really providing, you can be overtaken by competitors or by changing buying habits. The Swiss watch industry, for example, has fought back with companies such as Swatch stealing a march by promoting watches as fashion accessories. What business are they in now?

Getting the product or service right is all about making sure it satisfies customers' needs or wants and can be produced and delivered at a profit. There are an enormous number of ways you can make your product different and more appealing. The sort of factors you could consider are: Does it look right, feel right and how well does it do the job? What special features does it have and how do those translate into benefits that customers need and/or want? Is it attractive enough, both visually and functionally, to appeal to sufficient customers (you'll want to sell in reasonable volumes even if you have chosen to adopt a focus strategy) in preference to the offerings from competitors? Is it appropriately and attractively packaged? How reliable is it? Does it meet the expectation of the target market in terms of perceived quality and value for money?

Even if you sell a tangible product, the associated service is a very important part of what customers buy. Service factors to think about include: Is there appropriate back-up? Are the instructions clear? Are you able to offer the sort of delivery, lead-time and installation service the customer requires? Are the payment terms appropriate to customers' needs and wants?

How will you make your business different? There has to be something unique either about you or your product that makes you stand out from your competitors. It could be something as obvious as being open later, longer. Or it may be a policy, such as the John Lewis Partnership's 'never knowingly undersold' message. In the case of a product, you may be able to manufacture it to a higher quality than competing products.

Markets are dynamic – they do not stand still; customer requirements and expectations change over time. Consequently, you also need to think about trends and their potential effect on the future development of your product or service: What are the future trends? What is the potential impact on product or service specification? What needs will customers have in the future? What benefits will they be seeking in tomorrow's products?

You need to be totally clear about what you are hoping to sell. If you cannot describe it easily, then you will have difficulty selling it. Equally, you have to be clear about it before you do your market research.

Once you know what you are selling and to whom, you can match the features of your product (or service) to the benefits that your customers will receive (or perceive that they will receive) when they purchase.

In addition, think about people who are not customers. What are their needs? What benefits are they seeking? Have you missed out on becoming their supplier because of a mismatch between what you have to offer and what they want to buy?

Industry attractiveness

In Chapter Two, the concept of market segmentation was introduced as a way of defining your specific market place more accurately. If you are selling in more than one segment then you might find it helpful to consider the *attractiveness* and *competitive position* of each segment.

General Electric, who not only sold in a number of different segments, but also in many totally different business sectors, have developed a matrix to help them assess which subsidiaries to expand, which to retain and which to sell by plotting the position of each subsidiary according to industry attractiveness and competitive position (Figure 5.3). An industry might be attractive because there are no or few competitors, or because margins are high, or because customers have to buy the product, etc. Your competitive position may be strong because your costs are low compared to your competitors, or because you have unique strengths, competences and skills, etc.

For example, you sell computer hardware. The industry is not very attractive because of high competition and low margins. After analysing your strengths and weaknesses you conclude that you are weak compared to your competitors. As a result you place that service in the bottom right hand corner.

On the other hand, you also write bespoke software for real time control applications. The market is small, but there is little competition and margins are high. You are strong compared to your competitors and so you place this service in the top left hand corner.

Do this for all your products and services. Aim to concentrate on those in the top left. Take care, however, before divesting. Do those low

FIGURE 5.3   GE Business screen

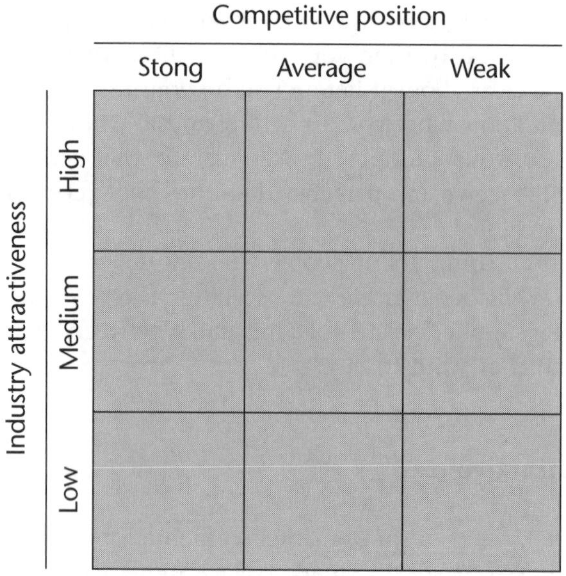

Competitive position

	Stong	Average	Weak

Industry attractiveness — High / Medium / Low

margin, highly competitive services carry a high burden of fixed costs? Do they promote your name to prospective customers?

Opportunities to grow

Almost certainly some, if not all, of your goals will be about growth or will require growth in order to achieve. Essentially, there are just four ways in which you can make your business grow bigger.

Even if you are not planning to grow just yet, looking ahead may be helpful in defining your marketing objectives and marketing mix. The matrix shows the four ways in which you can grow your business.

Market penetration

You may encourage existing customers to buy more through advertising, publicity and special promotions. You might win customers from your competitors by attractive pricing, aggressive advertising, seeking new distribution channels, etc.

FIGURE 5.4   Strategies for product/market developments

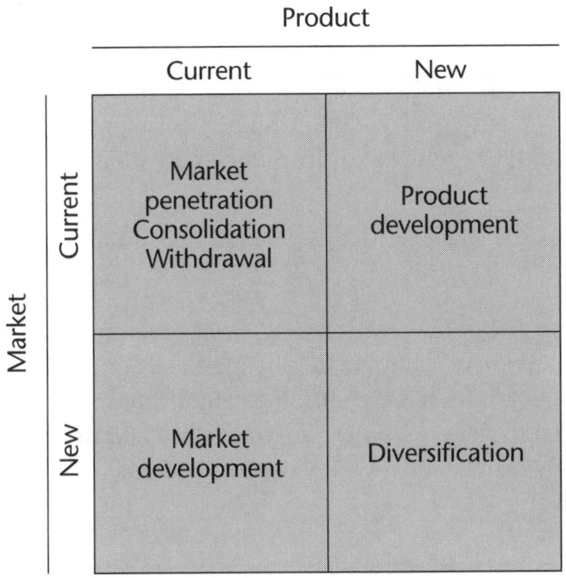

Source: Adapted from product/mission matrix (Ansoff, 1987)

You may discover that you are really struggling in a market and have difficulty competing. The most sensible strategy might simply be to withdraw from that market, perhaps at the same time identifying an appropriate diversification opportunity! Withdrawal will allow you to free up resources which can be used more profitably elsewhere. Before you do decide definitely to withdraw from a market, remember that your sales of that product in that market (assuming that you do have at least some sales) will still be making a contribution to your overheads. So you need to ensure that you have an alternative source of income.

Market development

This is where you introduce your current products to new markets – these might be different market segments, or new regions, or even new countries. This can be achieved through different distribution channels, advertising in different media, offering the product in slightly different ways to appeal to each new segment. For example, you might repackage financial software for banks for use by accountants.

Product development

This requires enhancement or development of existing products, or the addition of completely new products, but selling them to your existing markets. You might simply add new features, or possibly remove some features; you might add to your range, perhaps additional sizes or enhanced quality; or you might introduce new models.

Diversification

Diversifying is the hardest choice since this involves identifying opportunities for new products in new markets. For example, you might add new products which are technologically related to existing products, but will appeal to new customers; or you might add new products which are completely unrelated to your existing products.

Case study: Hydro Technologies Ltd

Hydro Technologies has established a good customer base in the UK. It is now aiming to expand internationally not just through exporting but also through the establishment of joint ventures, particularly in the Middle East. They know that there is a demand for cut marble. Their equipment is ideal since it is the only means of cutting marble without chipping or leaving burn marks.

Achieving your product/market strategy

Having determined the product/market development strategy, you need to consider the method you plan to use to develop the market or product. The most common method adopted by smaller businesses, often totally unconsciously, is simply organic growth – achieve more sales, take on more staff, set higher targets, and so on. As you grow, however, you may spot opportunities for growth through acquisition or some sort of strategic alliance or joint venture.

Case study: Xtralite Ltd

Xtralite manufactures roof lights, that is, windows for use in flat roofs. Its core business of roof lights grows as the demand for roof lights grows and as more customers understand that their quality is second to none – so it is pursuing organic growth in its core activity.

They have established a structural glazing division, which is primarily selling a new service to existing customers – pursuing organic growth through offering a new product. They have recently bought a distributor of windows – which provides growth by acquisition – and opens up new markets for their core products.

They believe that there is room for another manufacturer of roof windows, that is, windows for use in pitched roofs – that at least is the message they are getting from their existing customers. They plan to grow by developing and manufacturing a new product, in a joint venture, initially selling to existing markets but, they hope, quickly expanding into new markets also – growth by strategic alliance, providing new products and opening up new markets.

Conclusion

You don't necessarily need to have all, or indeed any, of this written down. It will probably help to have the purpose written down. You may even want to frame it and hang it on the wall. It will probably also help to write down your challenging goals, as a reminder of what lies ahead, to facilitate discussions with partners, colleagues and staff, to explain to funders, etc.

Remember the statement earlier that strategy is what helps you achieve your goals. As you progress towards your goals, you may need to change your chosen strategies. That doesn't matter. It's the goals that are important. You may enter new markets and find that you adopt different strategies to compete. You may utilize different methods in order to enter different markets.

If you have chosen your purpose carefully, it is likely that this will not change, or only change slightly over time. If everything goes according to plan you will, of course, achieve your goals and will want to replace them with new goals. Do not have too many goals, otherwise you will be torn between which one to work on.

Aim to have complementary goals. For example, you may choose one goal about doubling turnover. A second goal might be to enter a foreign market. A third goal might be to launch a joint venture. These are all mutually reinforcing. You might also have a goal to develop a new product. Whilst this may be essential, it may also distract you from starting to export your current products.

You need to have a generic strategy, you need to think carefully about your product/market mix and which combination is appropriate for growth and you need to think about the relevant method to achieve that.

You will want, periodically, to review progress towards your goals and, if necessary, take corrective action to keep yourself on course. If you have thought about scenarios and milestones this will be fairly straightforward.

Lastly, remember the point about having fun and seeking rewards. Many people still see businesses as being about maximizing profit – and they talk about targets in terms of quantity – maximizing sales revenue or market share or profit. Arguably, however, a healthy company is one that, whilst recognizing the importance of profit, sees a wider role – in developing its staff or in community involvement for example – and so does not measure its success solely by looking at the bottom line.

TABLE 5.2   Strategic approaches

Generic	Product/market	Methods
Cost leadership	Market penetration	Internal growth
Differentiation	Product development	Acquisition
Focus	Market development	Strategic alliance
	Diversification	Joint venture
	Withdrawal	

Source: Adapted from Johnson and Scholes (1993).

CHAPTER SIX

Defining objectives and measuring performance

Planning for success

Strategic thinking will help you to define your purpose, goals and overall direction. It will give you an overarching framework which provides guidance as you manage your business. The strategy sets out purpose, philosophy, our key areas of activity and, for each activity area, a small number of audacious or challenging goals. Whilst it may be helpful to write this down, many businesses progress quite happily with it all in the mind of the proprietor. There is a need for every business, however, to plan and agree shorter term objectives and targets.

In this chapter, we will look at how those policy objectives can be quantified as strategic objectives and, perhaps more importantly, how strategic objectives can be operationalized. In setting specific objectives you may need to take account of specific strategic requirements such as driving up quality, or spreading risk by focusing on more than one market, or the ethical requirements of your customers. Operational objectives need associated performance measures, which can then be used as the standard against which performance, and progress, can be measured. Success in achieving those shorter term operational objectives – think of it as success in managing your resources – demonstrated by meeting the targets, will, in due course, lead to success in achieving the strategic objectives and, thus, the audacious goals. Setting short-term targets requires more detailed planning.

A sound planning process will:

- ensure all objectives fall within the business's strategic aims;

- identify measurable objectives, which can be clearly demonstrated when fulfilled;

- break each objective down into sub-objectives and tasks, which include timescales for completion;

- analyse each task against the likely barriers which may either prevent it from being done or create delays or problems in completing it;

- consider the ways that barriers can be either prevented from occurring or dealt with when they arise;

- monitor progress regularly and evaluate the success of each of the business's actions.

Getting down to numbers

It has been said that if you can't measure it, you can't manage it. But what, exactly, is it that you want to measure? Well, that partly depends on the goals and strategic objectives that you set. Once you have defined your strategic direction you will need to set long-term objectives, such as product introduction, diversification, geographic expansion and market penetration. (Introduce a new product in each of the next three years; develop a joint venture in order to enter a new market; start exporting to the Far East; have 30 per cent of the local market within 6 years.) These will then need to be broken down into short-term achievable objectives (such as increase in market share of 5 per cent per annum). Setting overall objectives is more difficult, therefore, than simply stating that the objective is to operate without making a loss or to maximize profits. Defining objectives and targets will provide the basis for monitoring overall performance and in measuring progress. Some large companies set themselves targets expressed as ratios for example, sales per employee, profit per employee, return on equity, net profit margin, etc. What is possible will differ between sectors. Capital intensive businesses, such as banks or property companies, may perform well measured on profit per employee, but badly measured on return on equity. Service sector businesses, with less equity, show a better return on equity, but may make less profit per employee.

When considering possible performance measures, you may find it helpful to use these MEASURE criteria:

- *matched* – measures should be benchmarked or compared with others so that you have an idea of an acceptable target and acceptable tolerance;

- *equitable* – measures should be balanced;

- *aligned* – measures should be aligned with the overall strategy;

- *simple* – measures used should require simple data collection and analysis and the result should be simple to understand;

- *united* – measures should be linked across the different objective areas;

- *responsible* – measures need to be quantitative so that people can be held accountable;

- *essential* – only use the measures that are of critical importance rather than having too many.

Many people think of strategic objectives purely in terms of finance. But that is not enough. Almost certainly, you will have defined your purpose in terms of product and market, so in setting specific objectives, this is probably a good place to start. I manage a so-called 'non-profit organization'. They are badly named. Like any other company we need to make a profit – but that profit is all ploughed back into our work rather than being distributed to shareholders. Non-profit organizations are often better than the for-profit sector, however, at setting strategic objectives beyond finance and marketing.

Peter Drucker (1974) echoes this thinking, noting the importance of setting non-economic objectives, particularly regarding staff development. He argues that there are eight key areas in which objectives should be set and against which performance should be measured. His list covers:

- market standing;

- innovation;

- human organization including manager performance and development, staff performance and attitude;

- productivity;

- financial resources;

- physical resources;

- profitability;

- social responsibility.

Jack Welch, CEO of America's General Electric, on the other hand advocates setting performance measures in just three areas:

- customer satisfaction;

- staff satisfaction;

- cash flow.

The trick in all of this is to achieve an appropriate balance between the different sets of objectives.

The balanced scorecard

Robert Kaplan, of the Harvard Business School and David Norton, of Renaissance Solutions Inc, have developed further the idea that you must have more than just financial objectives and created what they call the 'balanced scorecard' (Kaplan and Norton, 1992). They were concerned that too many senior managers were simply focusing on financial measures like return on investment and earnings per share. Some people responded to this by looking for more sophisticated financial measures; others decided to ignore financial measures and concentrated on, say, quality measures. Kaplan and Norton assert that you cannot afford to rely on just a single set of measures, but need an appropriate balance.

They suggest that businesses adopt goals and performance measures in four areas:

- finance (with particular thoughts about shareholders' views);

- marketing (how is the business seen by customers);

- continuous improvement (how can the business continue to improve and innovate);

- an internal view looking at excellence (in which I would include staff development).

Kaplan and Norton argue that the scorecard puts vision and strategy, rather than control, at the centre. It can be used to help businesses focus and agree on the strategic objectives necessary across all four areas in order to achieve their 'big hairy audacious goals'. Use of a technique such as this can also ensure that the processes of strategic planning, resource planning and budgeting are consistent. Hopefully, people will then take appropriate action to move the business towards achieving those objectives – the measures are intended to give an

FIGURE 6.1   Goals and performance measures in four key areas

Financial perspectives		Customer perspectives	
Goals	Measures	Goals	Measures
• Survive • Succeed • Grow • Prosper	• Profitability • Acceptable level of gearing • Level of retained earnings • Liquidity • Shareholder satisfaction	• Reputation • Value for money • New markets • Outperform competitors	• Customer delight • Level of repeat business • Word of mouth recommendations • Customer complaints

Internal perspectives		Improvement perspectives	
Goals	Measures	Goals	Measures
• Reputation • Staff competence • More effective R&D	• Staff morale • Staff satisfaction • Staff turnover • Level of personal development activity • Financial ratios relating to staff costs	• Efficiency • Effectiveness • Economy • New products • Public image	• Product innovation • Process innovation • Reduction in failure rate • Reduction in scrap rate • Community satisfaction

indication of how well the business is doing in progressing towards those objectives.

This does require, of course, that you quantify the gap between where you want to be and where you are now. Benchmarking may be helpful: How are other businesses performing? What can you learn from them? But irrespective of how other businesses are doing you will almost certainly want to set objectives which stretch and challenge – in order to help you to keep developing and growing. You can then set performance measures which start to move you in that direction.

Choosing appropriate strategic objectives

Whilst you will need to make up your own mind about the areas in which to define strategic objectives, I have found it helpful to consider them under five headings:

- business activities;

- marketing;

- finance;

- quality;

- staff development.

Ideally you will require a minimum of one and a maximum of around three long-term objectives under each of those headings. If you have too many, it is unlikely that you will be able to make progress on all of them simultaneously.

You may find it helpful, in setting your objectives, to think about the three or four critical success factors for your business – and then concentrate on ensuring that those are delivered.

Critical success factors

- Yeoman Pressings believe that this means customer service – looking after customers and providing them with the best possible service.

- PI Engineering, who provide structural steelwork to the construction industry, also want to provide customer service – in their case through problem solving, in the form of architectural and technical guidance, backed up by quality of work.

- Hydro Technologies stress customer service, providing technology flexibility to enable the customer to meet their requirements – which they achieve through employing the right staff and investing heavily in research and development.

- Andrews Plastics believe a competitively priced one stop shop service is what keeps them ahead.

- Flexible Learning Associates see organization and enthusiasm as their critical success factors.

Your overall strategy and your critical success factors are interdependent – being competitively priced implies a cost leadership strategy; having enough money to invest heavily in research and development, or having the time to problem solve, implies a strategy of differentiation. Setting individual strategic objectives, and operational objectives, will provide you with key performance indicators – against which you can measure performance and progress. Remember though that measures are there to underpin your goals. They are intended to help you control your business. Think back to the Plan-Do-Check-Act cycle. Measures help you to check performance and give you the means to exercise control – they should not become goals in themselves.

Furthermore, measures do not tell you how to achieve the goals. Do not forget the human dimension to achieving your goals, which we will look at in some detail in the next chapter.

Business activities

If you've managed to read this far without defining your business activity, perhaps now would be a good time to consider it. Think carefully about what business you want to be in. Remember the story about Ronson and Parker being more in the gift business than the lighter business or the pen business. Whilst they still choose to constrain, to a certain extent, the specific products that they make, the business definition helps them with how they position themselves in the market place and with their marketing. Careful definition of your business activity may affect exactly what it is that you actually do. The Burton Group is seen by customers as suppliers of clothes – but, as described earlier, they see themselves as designers and marketers.

In defining what it is that you want to do, you too will want to think about your core competences as well as your resource availability. Is your strength in design? Is it in marketing? Is it in manufacturing? If you focus on a small part of the total process in getting your product or service to your customers, how easy will it be to sub-contract the rest of the process?

In any event, you may find that concentrating on just a part of the process requires less resources and so there could be good financial reasons for such focus as well.

Break down the entire process of getting your product or service to customers into as many individual activities as possible and think carefully about whether you must keep control of it to remain competitive – it doesn't matter at this stage whether you want to keep doing it or not. The objective is simply to identify those activities that give you a competitive edge. If you are a sub-contract machine shop or electronics assembly plant, you will want your manufacturing process to be as efficient as possible – because the competition largely competes on price. If you are manufacturing your own product, you will be concerned to protect your design ability. You may have a novel approach to marketing – or you may be able to sub-contract some or all of it to others.

Crucially, once you have decided on your core competence, you can consider how you can build on that. Suitable objectives might include product innovation (new product every year) or process innovation (reduce cost of manufacturing) or diversification.

It can be difficult to separate the big hairy audacious goals – diversification into a new product targeting a new market, say – from the operational goal – acquisition or joint venture, say – needed to achieve it. Diversification could be achieved, albeit more slowly, through organic growth. You may nevertheless find it helpful to separate ends and means. In this case the end is diversification and the means is the joint venture. If you have a clear idea of the end, then you will be more rigorous when seeking and reviewing the means.

If joint venture or acquisition is attractive, you will need to have available the wherewithal to fund it. At an early stage in your strategic thinking, you may want to start building up cash reserves by ensuring a healthy level of retained earnings. You will also need to ensure you are generating sufficient earnings to cover the research and development associated with product and process innovation.

Marketing objectives

Marketing starts with the customer (identifying their needs and aspirations) and ends with the customer (satisfying those needs.) Arguably, therefore, marketing should also be concerned with everything in between. Certainly, you need to ensure that you are aware of customer needs and are able to meet those needs to the satisfaction (or more) of the customer. But what do you measure in order to get a feel for how well you are performing? Looking at big business approaches gives few clues – they are often hung up on too many measures.

It is difficult to define a boundary between activities and marketing. Since businesses should be market driven, responding to the needs of their customers, this is not really a problem. Customers buy benefits – if the features of the product do not confer the benefit sought by customers, then they will not buy. This will help you define your areas of activity. You then need to persuade customers to pay a price for those benefits which is greater than the cost to you of providing the features. And there need to be enough customers buying sufficient products to cover all your costs and generate a profit.

Strategic objectives for marketing and business activity, therefore, are probably best considered as one. And these will be largely defined by your overall goals and direction. So marketing objectives might better be considered as medium- to long-term objectives (say beyond a year or two) and short-term objectives (say for the year ahead). Medium-term objectives might include, for example:

- level of sales (to achieve sales of £1m this year and £1.25m next year);

- increase in sales (to grow sales by 25 per cent per annum);

- market share or increase in market share (to achieve market share of 25 per cent within three years).

Short-term objectives will typically be what you put in your business plan for the year ahead. These might include:

- level of profit (to generate 9 per cent net profit margin);

- return on investment or return on equity (to achieve 17 per cent return on capital employed);

- level of productivity or improvement in productivity (to achieve 10 per cent more output with no increase in fixed costs).

It is rarely sufficient to set just one of these indicators as an objective. It may well be easier to run a business with a turnover of £1m and 20 per cent net profit than one with a turnover of £2m and 10 per cent net profit.

Short-term measures such as these may still be regarded as too far removed from everyday tasks, so think about the specific tasks that need to be achieved. The return on investment will require additional sales. Additional sales and increased productivity will both help profitability. Your sales target might therefore increase from 1000 units to 1200 units. Break that down into monthly targets. Set key milestones. Review your performance regularly. Take corrective action if required.

Setting the overall targets is the easy part. You then have to do whatever is necessary to achieve them. In the example above, you might use the pyramid: sales of 1200 units requires, say, 4800 enquiries – which, in turn, requires distribution of 48,000 promotional leaflets.

A key part of the marketing strategy of any business is defined by the way you position yourself in the market place as described earlier. This is then supported by your choice of marketing mix – the 4Ps of product, price, place and promotion.

Choice of product and price tend to have strategic implications; place and promotion are more likely to be covered by operational objectives. Place is used as a synonym for distribution, otherwise there wouldn't be 4Ps! Distribution is about ensuring that your product or service is available in the right place at the right time. It is about ensuring that you have the right distribution channels. Think carefully about how you currently distribute your product or service. Are there ways in which you can improve? Is there scope to cut costs?

Promotion, particularly if you are following a strategy of differentiation, is the most important one of the 4Ps. It ensures that you communicate effectively with prospective customers so that they are encouraged to make a purchasing decision in your favour. Promotion might include advertising, tele-sales, face to face selling, etc. You will want to set a number of targets and to measure performance to determine which methods, or mix of methods, are most effective. If you choose to advertise, for example, you will want to monitor carefully how many responses you get and how many of those turn into sales. Then you can determine if it is a cost effective method. You may also want to review occasionally how well the method communicates with potential customers – what is their level of awareness – even if they are not stimulated to make an enquiry at the time.

Ideally you want your marketing not just to raise customer awareness but to move you through the stages of trust, satisfaction – where customers are happy with you – commitment – where you get repeat business – and advocacy – where customers recommend you to other potential customers.

One way of assessing customer needs as well as reviewing how well you are getting your message across is to hold periodic 'focus groups'.

Large businesses are increasingly experimenting with ever more sophisticated – and expensive – ways of measuring their performance. These include measures that you might expect – like market share, customer satisfaction and brand profit – but also more obscure ones like brand awareness and brand value. Many people's ideas of marketing have been shaped by the manufacturers of so-called fast moving consumer goods (FMCG). Manufacturers of FMCGs believe that their customers worry about specification, quality, service and price. They also believe that a high brand awareness – say for Ariel or Mars Bars – is crucial.

Smaller businesses are not, and cannot be, in the same league. Whilst FMCG manufacturers may go for cost leadership (though tempered with the belief that they can achieve a modest premium in exchange for their brand name) smaller businesses will have to concentrate on differentiating themselves from their competitors in some other way.

What is important is ensuring a feel for the market – not just your perception of the market, or your perception of the market 3 years ago, but a real, up to date idea of market needs.

Setting financial objectives

Marketing objectives go hand in hand with financial objectives, so the business needs to set financial objectives which are clear and measurable. Finance is simply a resource to enable you to achieve your goals – so your financial objectives are largely there to provide short- to medium-term targets. Measuring performance against the targets enables you to exercise control and, if necessary, to take corrective action. (Remember the Plan-Do-Check-Act cycle.) In the same way that marketing is about managing a business's relationship with its external environment, effective financial control is about managing the internal environment: liquidity, solvency, efficiency and profitability. This requires accurate record keeping and an understanding of the figures. An effective way of drawing conclusions from the figures is through the use of ratios. Ratios have long been used to review the performance of individual businesses, to compare their performance over time and to compare their performance with other businesses. Large businesses use ratios, particularly return on capital employed, to define targets, though this is less common in small businesses.

Ratios can be used by all businesses to set targets. Small and medium enterprises will particularly benefit from the better understanding of the business's performance and will, therefore, be in a position to exercise effective control. Because financial ratios largely inter-relate, only a small number of ratios need to be used to keep the business on track, though the specific ratios may not be the same for every business.

Ratio analysis provides a valuable tool to monitor the performance of a business and to spot trends and patterns. Looking at ratios for a single year can be misleading but their use can be particularly effective when used to make comparisons with the same ratios from previous years' accounts and from the accounts of other businesses operating in a similar environment. Ratios are published for many business sectors and these can be used as a comparison (sometimes referred to as Industry Norms – see, for example, figures produced by the Centre for Interfirm Comparisons or ICC Business Publications).

Some businesses like to watch their performance by monitoring figures such as sales per employee, profit per employee or even added value per employee.

Christopher Bartlett and Sumatra Ghoshal (1995), writing in the *Harvard Business Review*, report that Ikea, the Swedish home furnishings store which operates in 20 countries and has total sales of over $5bn, abolished the company's budgeting system in 1992. It now relies on a set of simple financial ratios both for setting targets and monitoring performance.

Appropriate strategic objectives might include profitability targets such as return on capital employed:

- to achieve a gross profit margin of 67 per cent;

- to achieve a net profit margin of 10 per cent of sales;

- to achieve a return on capital employed of 18 per cent;

- to achieve a return on equity of 33 per cent.

For everyday purposes, however, targets need to be broken down so that they are more easily measured. Let us take profit for example. A profit target will probably be defined as an absolute level of profit in money terms, but how can a business easily monitor progress towards achieving the defined level of profit. Profit before interest and tax is not an easy figure to monitor daily or weekly; return on capital employed or return on investment is even harder. But breaking those down into simpler components provides a set of ratios which are easy to calculate; indeed, for users of computerized computing packages, such as those available from Sage Group plc, they are probably already provided or could be with a little bit of careful setting up of the system.

Profitability

The most important objectives are those concerned with profitability. You will want to ensure that your gross profit is sufficient to cover all your overhead costs, and generate an additional profit to retain within the business. You will also need to generate sufficient cash to repay any loans that might be outstanding.

Gross profit margin is one objective that should be set at the outset of the business and then closely monitored.

$$\text{Gross profit margin} = \frac{\text{gross profit}}{\text{sales}} \times 100\%.$$

If your gross profit margin starts to drop you might be paying too much for raw materials or you might be having to discount your sales price too much to achieve sales. Many businesses also set a target for net profit margin. This ratio uses profit before interest and tax (PBIT).

$$\text{Net profit margin} = \frac{\text{PBIT}}{\text{sales}} \times 100\%.$$

Obtaining published accounts for your competitors can reveal a great deal about their performance. Whilst it is often difficult to determine their gross profit margin, it is relatively easy to discover their net profit margin. You can use this to benchmark your performance.

If you save money at a building society or have investments in quoted companies, you will be interested in the return that you make on your money. This is usually expressed as a percentage of the amount invested, say, 10 per cent. In the same way, profitability ratios show how good your business is as an investment. Furthermore, both lenders and third party investors will want to know the overall return on capital, as an indication of the security of the investment as well as an indicator of how well the business is performing, by giving a comparison with what could have been achieved had the same sum of money been saved or invested on the stock market. Accountants and banks, depending on their preferences, may look at:

- return on capital employed (RoCE);

- return on equity (RoE);

- return on total assets (RoTA).

Whilst these are all slightly different ratios they are all, in some way, looking at the return on assets. It is important, however, to be clear which figures are being used to derive the ratio and to be consistent, otherwise comparisons will be meaningless.

$$\text{RoCE} = \frac{\text{PBIT}}{\text{CE}} \times 100\%.$$

Capital employed (CE) is usually defined to cover equity plus long-term borrowings. I suggest (particularly where short-term borrowings are high compared to long-term borrowing – often the case with a small business) that capital employed is interpreted to cover all loan finance.[1] RoCE is an excellent measure of profitability – but it needs to be used with care. Businesses in their early stages of development may have little or no profit. Businesses relying on older, depreciated equipment will generate a higher return on a given level of sales than businesses with newer, more sophisticated equipment, though the business with the newer equipment may have better long-term prospects. As ever, therefore, the trick is in knowing what you want to do and then setting and using performance targets as a way of managing and controlling the process.

Some financiers prefer to look at return on total assets (TA). If you define capital employed to include all borrowings as suggested above, total assets is equal to capital employed plus trade debtors.

$$RoTA = \frac{PBIT}{TA} \times 100\%.$$

A measure of how hard the assets of the business are being made to work is given by the asset turn or capital turnover. Ideally, use the average total assets for the period.

$$Asset\ turn = \frac{Sales}{TA}.$$

For a large British company the asset turn is typically 1.1 and the average RoTA is 15 per cent (Walsh, 1993). Larger companies, however, are likely to have cash and fixed assets forming a larger proportion of their balance sheet assets than a small business; the small business should, therefore, be able to achieve a better asset turn. Note that net profit margin multiplied by asset turn gives RoTA, so a small business aiming for a RoTA of 15 per cent might set targets for a net profit margin of 10 per cent and for an asset turn of 1.5. You too can set targets or sales and gross profit margin to achieve your desired targets of net profit margin and asset turn.

As we noted above, it is possible to split ratios down – to give a number of ratios that can be used on a day to day basis to monitor activities (Figure 6.2).

Ratio Tree

Note that RoE is equivalent to RoCE multiplied by the leverage. In turn, RoCE is equivalent to the net profit margin multiplied by the asset utilization. The figures on the right hand side of the tree provide evidence about the financial efficiency of the business. The left hand side of the

FIGURE 6.2 Ratio tree

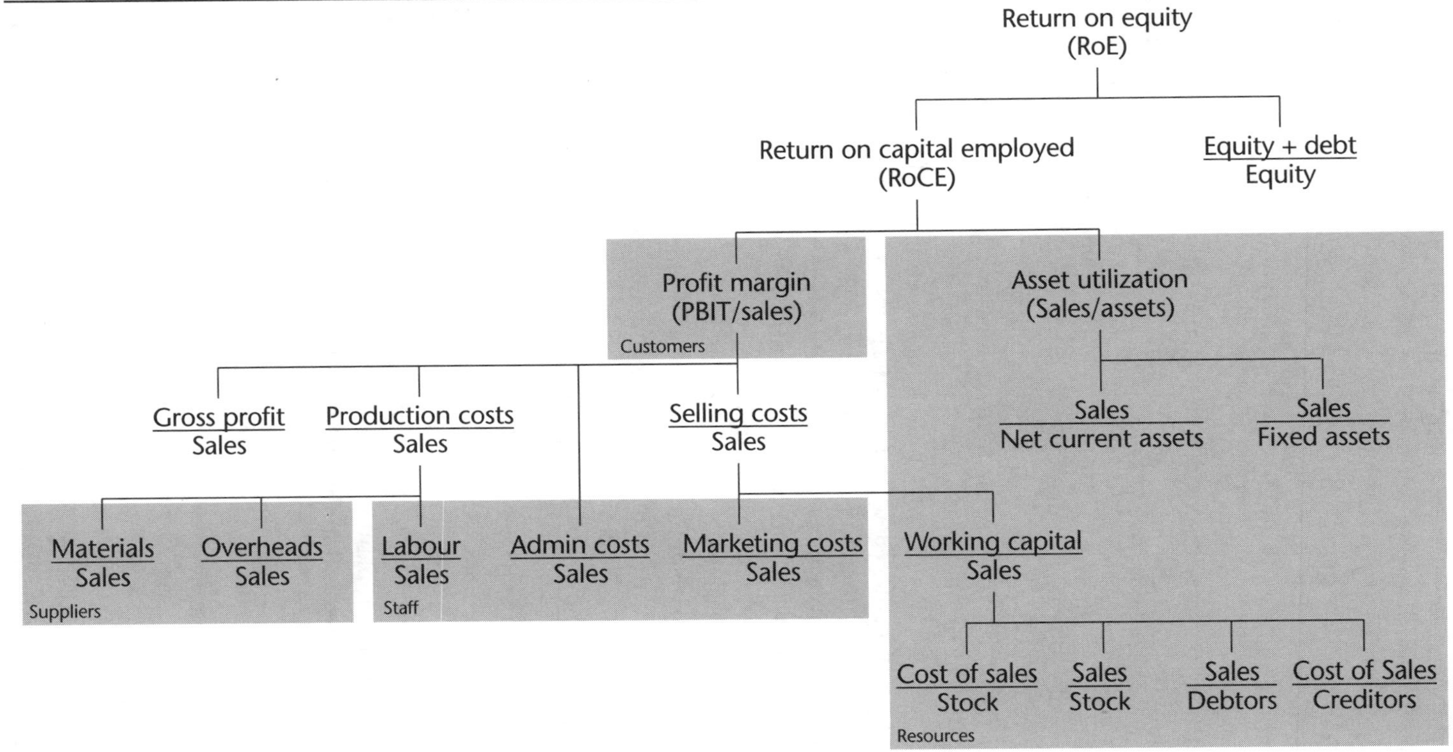

tree breaks down into a number of ratios, however, which will be of particular use in controlling costs on a day to day basis.

You can, if you wish, link the ratios to the stakeholders defined in the RSA's inclusive approach. How does each stakeholder contribute to your return on capital? Reducing staff absence or staff turnover, for example, or improving your reputation and satisfaction amongst customers, or reducing your overall cost of purchasing will all have a positive effect. Such actions may be obvious, but what is often less obvious is the need to think through the implications, particularly the human implications, of specific actions. Maintaining or improving your relationship with each of your stakeholders will help you to improve your return on capital.

If you are in manufacturing, then you are likely to have an investment in capital that is high compared to turnover. It makes sense, therefore, to pick suitable ratios to measure the return on capital. If part of the reason that you are in business is to create a job for yourself, or because you do not want to work for someone else, it is unlikely that you will be discouraged by a low return on your investment. It probably makes sense, therefore, to monitor the return on capital employed. In particular, this will provide you with good ammunition when you are negotiating with potential lenders or investors. Achieving your desired RoCE is a long-term, or strategic, objective.

Service businesses are not as likely to have so much capital tied up in fixed assets, though increasingly service businesses do find that they need heavy investment in information technology. They may also have capital tied up in premises. If you run a service business, you may think that it makes more sense to use staff performance ratios such as sales per employee or net profit per employee rather than profitability ratios based on capital returns.

You will also want to monitor your sales closely and ensure that you are achieving both the volume and the value targets. Achieving these targets, and keeping costs within their targets, will ensure that you achieve the return on capital or the staff performance that you have set.

If you are planning capital expenditure or want to pursue a joint venture or acquisition then you will need to consider the effect this might have on profitability and on cash flow. You might want to target a certain level of retained earnings each year, for example.

Gearing

Banks frequently talk about gearing and, usually in the same breath, state that they do not like to see businesses with a gearing greater than 50 per cent. New businesses, however, often have a gearing considerably higher than 50 per cent. Many businesses, as they grow larger, choose to set a gearing objective or have one imposed by the bank as a condition of lending.

Gearing is normally defined as the ratio of debt (i.e. loans from all sources including debentures, term loans and overdraft) to the capital employed. The higher the proportion of loan finance, the higher the gearing.

$$\text{Gearing} = \frac{\text{loans} + \text{bank overdraft}}{\text{equity} + \text{loans} + \text{bank overdraft}}.$$

If cash flow is stable and profit is fairly stable, then you can afford a higher gearing to benefit the equity investors.

Effect of gearing

The gearing of a business can have an important effect on the return achieved on capital. Let us look at a simple example. Ignoring the effect of taxation, Company A has £20,000 capital employed, all of which is equity, and makes a profit of £5,000. RoCE is, therefore, 25 per cent. RoE is also 25 per cent. (RoE is the ratio of profit after tax (PAT) to equity.)

Company B has £20,000 capital employed; half is equity and half is borrowed from the bank at 12½ per cent. It, too, makes a profit of £5,000 so RoCE is still 25 per cent. Interest reduces the profit to £3,750 giving an RoE of 38 per cent, dramatically higher than company A.

Company C also has £20,000 capital employed, but in this case just £2,000 is equity and £18,000 is borrowed, again at 12½ per cent. Its profit of £5,000 still gives an RoCE of 25 per cent. Interest reduces the profit to £2,750 but this is now a substantial 138 per cent RoE.

If the RoCE falls below the cost of borrowing money then the leverage works in the other direction.

Company D has £20,000 capital employed all of which is equity. It makes a profit of £2,000. The RoCE is 10 per cent and, in this case, so is the RoE.

Company E has £20,000 capital employed of which half is a loan at 12½ per cent. Profit before interest of £2,000 is reduced to £750 after interest of £1250 is deducted to give an RoE of 8 per cent.

Company F has £20,000 capital employed of which £18,000 is a loan at 12½ per cent. It makes a profit of £2,000 also giving an RoCE of 10 per cent, but it is in real trouble. Its interest amounts to £2,250 giving an overall loss of £250.

As a result equity investors, who will not have to contribute to losses, will want gearing as high as possible to benefit from the leverage effect of an RoCE higher than the cost of borrowing money. Conversely lenders, worried about the opposite leverage effect and the ability of a business to pay its interest charges, will want the gearing as low as possible.

You may also hear the term, leverage, though it is more commonly used in the USA. It gives an indication of how effectively the owners' equity has been at 'levering' loan finance.

$$\text{Leverage} = \frac{\text{Equity} + \text{loans} + \text{bank overdraft}}{\text{equity}}.$$

Liquidity ratios

Provided sales targets are achieved and costs are controlled, then the business will achieve its objectives for profitability. It is important, also, to keep a close eye on cash and working capital since it is quite possible to run out of cash even when a business is apparently extremely profitable. Two ratios in particular will assist in monitoring working capital.

A business should always have enough current assets (e.g. stock, work in progress, debtors, cash in the bank and so on) to cover current liabilities (e.g. bank overdraft, creditors and so on). Liquidity ratios indicate the ability of the business to meet liabilities with the assets available. The current ratio shows the relationship of current assets to current liabilities.

$$\text{Current ratio} = \frac{\text{current assets}}{\text{current liabilities}}.$$

This ratio should normally be between 1.5 and 2. If it is less than 1 (i.e. current liabilities exceed current assets) you could be insolvent. A stricter test of liquidity is the quick ratio or acid test. Some current assets, such as work in progress and stock, may be difficult to turn quickly into cash. Deducting these from the current assets gives the quick assets.

$$\text{Quick ratio} = \frac{\text{quick assets}}{\text{current liabilities}}.$$

The quick ratio should normally be around 0.7–1. To be absolutely safe, the quick ratio should be at least 1, which indicates that quick assets exceed current liabilities. If you are unable to pay your debts as they fall due then you are considered to be trading whilst insolvent which is an offence. It is essential, therefore, to ensure that you have sufficient working capital.

Economic value added

The current vogue measurement is economic value added (EVA) devised and promoted by American consultant, Stern Stewart (undated).

Some large businesses regard cash flow and cash management as important – on the basis that cash coming into the business enables bills to be paid on time and that, provided the targets have been set correctly, generating cash will generate profit. As a result, businesses are increasingly using measures such as economic value added (EVA) or cash flow return on investment (CFRoI).

The concept of added value is very simple – the price of the products or services that you sell equals the cost of the bought-in materials and services plus the value that you have added. The major element of added value is the work input by you and your staff. Added value is the cost of the labour input, together with the attributable proportion of overheads plus your profit. To put it another way, added value represents the amount by which your business has contributed to the creation of the country's wealth. Added value is effectively shared between four parties: the owners (through dividends), the staff (through wages), reinvestment (through retained earnings) and the government (through taxes).

Case study: Fulprint

Bob Scrase, who runs Fulprint, a printing business based in York, uses the concept of added value to assist his sales reps to maximize profit for the business. As he notes, his sales reps can always make a sale by dropping the price. There is a danger, however, that the gross profit margin falls too low to cover the overheads. To combat this, the sales reps' commission is now governed by their added value performance, rather than by their total sales performance.

Whilst calculating added value was easy for the computer, it was not so easy for the sales reps to understand! So Fulprint introduced a modification, such that all jobs are categorized into added value bands.

The target added value is 65 per cent of sales price. For each 5 per cent achieved over this target, the sales rep receives additional commission of 2 per cent of sales price, giving a likely maximum of 8 per cent on top of the normal commission of 5 per cent of sales price.

Added value can be used as a measure of efficiency. For example, added value per employee can be used to measure labour efficiency. The ratio of added value to wages gives a measure of staff productivity. The ratio of added value to capital employed gives an indication of capital productivity.

EVA goes further. The objective in calculating EVA is to give a feel for shareholder value. Shareholders want to maximize the total return (capital growth plus dividends) on their investment. For small businesses, who do not have external shareholders, or where shares are not easily traded, it will be difficult to realize any capital growth. EVA does help to assess performance, however, by showing whether the business is adding value or destroying it. EVA, in effect, says that a company is worth today the value of its future cash returns after allowing for the cost of capital, that is, the return required by investors and lenders on their money. If the cash return is greater than the cost of capital, the company will increase shareholder value; if the cash return is less, the company destroys value. EVA simply takes the operating profit after tax and deducts the real cost of all the capital employed. Not surprisingly, EVA will grow if profits can be increased without increasing the capital employed, or if additional capital can be invested and produce a return greater than the cost of that additional capital, or if existing capital can be re-employed in some more profitable activities. If a company does not make a reasonable margin over its cost of capital then arguably, as with RoCE earlier, it should be investing its funds elsewhere. It is, if you like, a measure of the wealth created (that is, the value added) by the company. It would be possible to do a simple calculation straight from the accounts, but, significantly, in calculating EVA it is necessary to adjust many of the accounting entries to give an economic value. It is now normal accounting practice, for example, to write off expenditure on research and development in the year in which it is incurred; it may, however, be more appropriate in terms of measuring added value to write it off over the lifespan of the product developed in order to reflect its economic life.

A key advantage of concentrating on cash flow measurement is that, unlike profitability measurement, it is harder to be creative with the accounts and so it is more reliable. A graphic example of such differences is Daimler Benz, which listed on the New York Stock Exchange in 1993. Under German accounting rules it was able to report a profit of $0.37bn, but under NYSE's rather tougher rules it had to report a loss of $1.1bn! (*The Economist*, 1997).

A further advantage of EVA is that it can be used as a measure for setting up staff bonus programmes. The Burton Group used to have a bonus system based on turnover. Store managers would buy in too much stock and then shift it in cut price sales. This was good for turnover but poor for profit (*Sunday Times*, 1995).

Resources

Chapter Four stressed the importance of resource management and suggested that success depends on how you manage your key resources of people, information and money. You need, therefore, to set appropriate targets for each of these. Your strategy or annual operating plan will highlight the key tasks and priorities.

From these you can prepare a resources plan. All of the tasks will require people and/or equipment – so you can devise a staff plan and a capacity plan. If you are introducing new products or new processes or researching new markets you will need a project plan. These all have financial implications – so you can prepare a budget. If you can afford the cost, well and good. If not you may have to go more slowly, or seek a strategic partner, or look for grant aid. As ever, you will need to monitor progress against the plan.

Capital investment

Earlier, it was noted that businesses should be seeking productive opportunities. Those opportunities may simply be for organic growth or may be for joint ventures or acquisitions. These will all require investment, often of substantial sums of capital. As part of your strategic framework, therefore, you may, like a larger business, wish to set a minimum expected return, often called a 'hurdle rate'. The absolute minimum hurdle rate will be the cost of capital or the opportunity cost if you already have the capital available, though most businesses then add a 'risk premium'.

There are a number of techniques available which you can use to assess whether you should invest in a particular project. They will help you to calculate the expected financial return, and then you can decide whether the return is sufficient to make the project attractive.

The reason for investing in a project is that, whilst it will cost you money in the short term, you expect to generate income in the future which will more than cover the original outlay. So appraisal techniques must comprise cash outflows now with expected future cash inflows. Appraisal techniques include:

- payback;

- return on capital employed;

- net present value;

- internal rate of return.

Whilst methods based on payback and return on capital employed are widely used and have advantages in some situations, net present value and internal rate of return give a more accurate assessment of the worth of a project.

This is not the place to discuss appraisal techniques in detail, but you may like to consider, as one of the elements of your strategic framework, the hurdle rate that you would seek before pursuing an investment opportunity.

Quality objectives

What is quality? Is it getting everything right 90 per cent of the time, or 99 per cent, or 99.99 per cent. London Heathrow has around 400,000 aircraft movements per year – so a 0.01 per cent failure rate would be 40 crashes! Needless to say they aim never to have a failure. The same is true for many other businesses. Yes, things will go wrong from time to time – the key difference is whether any level of failure is acceptable, or whether the target, like Heathrow, should be for no failure.

Deciding that quality is of particular importance is a strategic decision. The decision, for example, to introduce total quality management will have an effect on your overall strategy – it will permeate everything you do. Total quality management is a state of mind. For most organizations, it requires a cultural shift and hard work to ensure that it is kept up – on the other hand, it will also help to bring focus to the needs of your customers and encourage everyone both to think about continuous improvement and about becoming a learning organization. A first step towards introducing total quality management might be achieving accreditation to ISO9000.

There are almost certainly some processes in your business for which you have procedures, even if those procedures are not written down. Imagine, for example, you are a software business. Trying to understand a programme a year after writing it could be very difficult, and all but impossible if a different person is trying to amend the code. So you require your programmers to prepare suitable documentation at the same time as they write the code. Or you may have procedures to ensure that your raw materials are of the right quality. Or to ensure that supplier invoices are checked against purchase orders. These are all examples of procedures. The best businesses have always used procedures – so that different members of staff can pick up, if necessary, part way through a process understanding what has already happened and knowing what needs to be done next. ISO9000 simply requires the use of procedures. They don't have to be complicated. They don't have to wrap the business in red tape. They simply require a level of consistency and documentation which will help you in the effective running of your business.

Introducing TQM and ISO9000 will probably identify training needs for your staff. On the other hand, ensuring that there are in place proper procedures to govern your activities will also make it easier when inducting and training new staff.

TQM is a way of planning and managing all the activities in an organization, to lead to a process of continuous improvement, through the prevention of potential problems, as well as the solving of existing ones. To be successful, the TQM approach must become embodied in the organizational culture. Quality must be designed and manufactured into the product. Inspection cannot add to the quality; it merely weeds out products which do not reach the appropriate standard. TQM brings quality awareness to everyone in your business, focusing on customers and their quality needs.

TQM is an opportunity to improve all business functions. The benefits of quality improvement include cost savings, staff commitment and increased confidence of what is required from each person in your business.

Through staff involvement at all levels of the business people want to do their job right first time, every time, which, after all, is what they are paid to do. This leads to reduced rework, reduced scrap levels, improved performance and, ultimately, higher levels of customer confidence and an enlarged customer base.

There are common elements within TQM and marketing. Both must begin and end with the customer. A good quality manager will understand the principles, if not the theories, of marketing and vice versa. The line between the two has become increasingly blurred but, in essence, marketing is finding out what the customer wants and offering it. TQM is ensuring that what the customer wants can be provided. Both disciplines call for large amounts of analysis and evaluation.

There are many reasons for wanting to improve quality. It can sometimes seem that the main one is to make life easier for your customers. But the biggest reason should be to have more control over your business. By continually improving all of the activities within your business, you will automatically reduce the level of failures too. Any kind of failure adds a cost to your business whether it is wasted materials or scrap, wasted time, lost opportunities of future business, or indeed frustration on behalf of your staff or yourself. So continually improving all the elements in your business is worthwhile for its own sake.

Thorough analysis of every process within a business inevitably leads to greater understanding. Observation of the conditions which lead to an ideal product or service being produced give businesses a target at which to aim. By recreating that ideal environment they can consistently produce the ideal product or service. In the same way, by analysing the conditions which lead to a poor service, companies can isolate and eliminate the factors which are creating the negative effect. Some businesses don't know why they are having problems, but by analysing the conditions under which problems occur, they may be able to identify the cause.

Businesses usually lose customers for one of three reasons:

- quality problems;

- price;

- unsatisfactory human relationships.

We are now in the era of the complete service business. Customers do not need to trade with people who will not offer them that little bit more. One of the more positive trends to emerge in recent years is the concept of 'complete customer satisfaction'.

The first requirement of the planning process is to think realistically about your quality objectives, which must be closely linked to your overall objectives. Why improve the quality of service to your customers if it won't increase the number of customers you have or reduce the level of complaints? Why become more efficient unless it enables you to reduce costs and re-direct resources from fault finding to looking for new business?

Quality objectives should not contradict the general aims of your business. Rather, quality objectives need to reflect the direction in which you want your business to move and support any existing plans for development.

Typical quality objectives

Here is a list of typical quality objectives – it is not exhaustive; nor will all of them will be applicable to your business, but it may give a starting point:

- increase customer satisfaction;
- reduce rework;
- introduce quality control;
- introduce staff training;
- encourage personal control of quality;
- undertake staff attitude surveys;
- reduce customer complaints;
- reduce product returns;
- reduce manufacturing costs;
- reduce scrap allowance;
- reduce bad debt;
- reduce staff turnover;
- improve information to workforce;
- introduce continuous improvement;
- keep up with technology;
- harness ideas from the shop floor;
- increase profits;
- introduce research and development;
- introduce recognized quality standards;
- introduce benchmarking;
- increase understanding of competitors;
- undertake market research;

- improve relations with suppliers;

- improve negotiation skills with staff and suppliers;

- increase knowledge of customer requirements;

- help customers to identify their own requirements;

- invest in new technology;

- undertake internal and external quality audits;

- introduce quality circles;

- begin ISO9000 process;

- reduce absenteeism;

- measure effectiveness of quality programmes;

- increase safety awareness;

- increase environmental awareness;

- introduce staff appraisal;

- introduce better customer documentation;

- undertake statistical analysis.

By describing a situation which will exist once an objective has been fulfilled, you can ensure your objectives are likely to be achieved. For example, if your objective is to increase customer satisfaction in the next year, how would you know if you had succeeded?

You could say that 'in response to a customer care survey undertaken in January, at least 90 per cent of clients will respond with an overall score of at least 4 (on a scale of 1–5)'.

Each objective you set must include in its description factors which can be measured, observed and verified. It is clearly pointless having objectives which you cannot measure, as you will never know whether you have achieved them.

Objectives should have as many definable criteria as possible. So dates, times, quantities, percentages, proportions and test results may all form part of a quality objective.

Bearing these thoughts in mind draft out your quality objectives. A typical list might be:

- Within six months – reduce complaints to less than 1 complaint per 100 sales.

- Within 12 months – reduce raw material wastage to 5 per cent of raw material costs.

- Improve utilization of machines from 55 per cent of capacity to 75 per cent by the end of next year.

There is a limit to how 'right' your quality can be if you do not involve suppliers. Many successful manufacturing businesses have created supplier partnerships where the level of trust and communication between buyer and seller is legendary. Nissan UK include supplier managers and staff in their internal training sessions. The trust apparent between businesses who operate just-in-time (JIT) buying policies and their suppliers is immense. If a large company has a single supplier for one component, the customer is depending on that supplier's ability to produce the goods. If the customer has to go to another supplier because of a breakdown with the usual vendor, how many other suppliers will be capable, let alone willing, to supply specific items at incredibly short notice? The message from these supply chains is clear, if you want a customer to guarantee you business you must develop a level of trust and communication between you which is absolutely transparent. Don't leave your suppliers to attempt to second-guess your needs – tell them what you want. If they can't supply what you want, find other suppliers.

Purchasing

At first glance, purchasing may not be regarded as a major issue. But it is one that it is rapidly growing in importance, especially if you are going to deliver to your own customers that which you have promised and which meets your customers' quality requirements and your cost requirements. Increasingly, larger companies are striving to cut the number of suppliers with which they deal. Furthermore, they are increasingly engaging in 'partnership sourcing', that is, developing a more enduring relationship with their suppliers than is the norm in more traditional transactional purchasing. In partnership sourcing, larger companies enter into longer term contracts with their suppliers, guaranteeing a specified level of spend, but often demanding improvements in quality, delivery times, after sales service, etc. Whilst on the face of it, this may cost the purchaser more, there may well be savings in improved quality and in reduced transaction costs through not having to retender as often.

As a smaller business, it is unlikely that you will be able to engage in partnership sourcing in quite the same way as a larger business. But your purchasing decisions may be just as critical for the success of your business. And whether your own strategy is one of differentiation or cost leadership, keeping both the cost of your purchases and your transaction costs under control is one of the best ways of ensuring that you remain profitable.

Have a look at your own purchases.

Non-critical supplies are low cost with plenty of competing suppliers and, consequently, changes in supplier will have little impact on your expenditure or your quality.

Leverage occurs where it is possible to group a number of non-critical suppliers together – to achieve better discounts and, possibly, less paperwork.

Critical supplies may be relatively low cost, but goods or services may be more difficult to obtain – such as software for an obsolescent computer system.

Strategic purchasing covers those goods or services which are both a higher proportion of your expenditure and also more difficult to obtain. This is where you need to work hard to manage your supplier relationships (Figure 6.3).

FIGURE 6.3   Purchases management

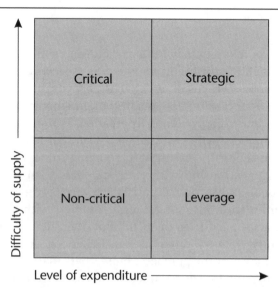

Conclusion

Strategic objectives have the danger of being too far removed from everyday reality for people to keep them in mind as they work. They also tend to be set for the medium to long term, rather than for the short term.

It is essential therefore not only to define strategic objectives but also to break them down into clear and explicit operational objectives with timescales, performance measures and targets. The operational objectives may simply be milestones along a route towards achieving a strategic objective – for example, introducing a quality improvement programme on the way to introducing Total Quality Management. They should always provide quantitative and/or qualitative targets so that performance can be measured.

As with the vision, operational objectives should be challenging, achievable and measurable. Don't have too many operational objectives, otherwise they become difficult to monitor. And remember to think about the assumptions on which your strategy is based.

Performance measures and targets enable the organization both to monitor its performance and the external environment and also to exercise control. Exercising control effectively requires the business to be able to measure its activities, to compare its activities with pre-determined criteria and to be able to adjust its activities in order to achieve the desired results. Organizations need continually to monitor themselves and the environment in which they are operating and, in response, modify their objectives, their plans and their budgets as necessary. At regular intervals, part of the corrective action will include modifying both operational objectives and strategic objectives.

A key component of achieving your strategy, however, will centre on your staff – and that is the topic of the next chapter.

Note

1 This definition is consistent with that used by Datastream, a major provider of company financial information in the UK.

CHAPTER SEVEN

Managing for success

Your most important asset

Throughout this book, we have noted the importance of the human aspects of business development. The best strategic intentions will come to nought if you and your team of staff are unable to implement them effectively. Businesses that perform consistently well are those that manage effectively the links between people, strategy and customers. It is important, therefore, to think carefully about how you lead, stimulate, manage and enthuse your staff so that they all pull in the same direction and so that they all give of their best. Once upon a time, senior managers aimed to ensure a uniformity of action amongst more junior staff, eliminating personal initiative. Now senior managers are far keener to harness personal initiative and entrepreneurship and to develop their staff for the good of the business.

You need to lead and to motivate – so that everyone who works with you is as keen and enthusiastic as you are to achieve the goals set for the business. If the business meanders, then the staff become demoralized, and then little works first time, and growth is slow or non-existent. A strong leader on the other hand, who can achieve agreement on a direction and then goes for it will eliminate the tendency to meander.

As your business grows, you will want to put in place a structure which both enables and encourages senior managers to be entrepreneurial themselves. Percy Barnevik, boss of Asea Brown Bovery has split the company into units averaging around 50 staff in order to encourage ABB 'to be simultaneously global and local, big and small, centralized and decentralized'.

Robert Waterman (1994) suggests that top performing companies take particular care over their organizational arrangements. They meet the needs of their people to attract better staff than their competitors and to motivate them effectively; and they meet the needs of their customers – through anticipation and innovation. Waterman notes that whilst this may sound simple, it actually requires an understanding of what motivates people and then ensuring a consistency between culture, structure, people and leadership all designed to motivate.

People

People are important to every business. No matter how automated a business, people are needed to keep the automation working and, far more importantly, people are needed at the interface with customers and the business's other stakeholders. It is essential, therefore, that staff – all staff – recognize the importance of their role in ensuring that customers receive excellent service. Whilst many businesses state that their staff are important, they do not always demonstrate that belief in practice. Treat them as being important. After all, your business depends on their skills, experience, motivation and morale.

It may help to have an understanding of what your staff are after and what motivates them. You may have thought already about their shared values. Robert Waterman suggests that there are five key factors:

- *control* – being able to determine, as far as possible, one's own actions;

- *shared vision* – they want something to believe in and to feel that they are making a difference;

- *challenge* – they want the thrill of stretching themselves to overcome challenges;

- *learning* – they want to develop themselves throughout their lives;

- *recognition* – they want to be appreciated for what they have achieved.

This is recognized in the DTI's Winning Companies report which notes that winning companies unlock the potential of their people through 'creating a culture in which employees are genuinely empowered and focused on the customer' and through 'investing in people through good training, learning and communications'.

All staff have talents – and the more these can be developed and exploited, the more successful will be the business. Everyone wants to perform to, or to surpass, their potential. So all you need to do is to harness that desire. That requires you to think about

- change and the effect of change likely to occur as you aim to make the business grow and how you can manage that change successfully and to the benefit of all;

- how to get the best out of your staff;

- an appropriate organizational structure;

- how to encourage personal learning and development which will not only assist your staff to achieve their potential, but will provide the business with the competences it needs for its next stage of growth.

Case study: Yeoman Pressings

Yeoman Pressings is located in the West Midlands. It is a manufacturing company specializing in sheet metal fabrication and presswork. The company designs, manufactures and sells a range of its own products as well as undertaking sub-contract work. A subsidiary company specializes in tubular steel fabrications.

They have a formal policy statement in which they explain 'the key factor in the success of both companies is, and will continue to be, our people. We are committed to the creation of an environment within which people can develop their potential to the full and be involved in decision making processes within the business. This includes the provision of management development training, team leader supervisory training and operator skills training all within an appropriate workplace infrastructure.'

This is reinforced in their mission statement which, rather than describing what the company does, reinforces their commitment to their staff: by 'striving for future prosperity for all of our employees by providing the best possible service to all of our customers and by maximising the sales of our own products; and achieving this by the total involvement and participation of all employees.'

So you need to think carefully about how to make best use of your staff. How do you recruit them? How do you train them? How do you develop them? In particular, how do you develop managers? And most importantly of all, how do you develop yourself as an effective leader?

Earlier, it was noted that the over-riding characteristic of the environment in which we live and work is change. Businesses have not only to live with change but also to embrace it. This requires that businesses are lead by champions of change: leaders with the vision and determination to use change as an opportunity to focus on the needs and aspirations of future customers, not just tomorrow's customers but perhaps the next decade's customers. You, as leader of your business, will have its goals and strategy at the back of your mind all the time – keep staff development and motivation at the front.

You will also want a structure – and a culture – that can cope with change. In this chapter, we will concentrate on the people aspects of running a business – leadership, managing staff, managing change, teams and team building, and learning and personal development.

Leadership

As the business grows, you need to guide it safely through change and through the stages of growth described in Chapter One, but you need to do it in such a way that everyone feels that they are responsible. Remember the words of Lao Tzu, 'But of a good leader, who speaks little, when his task is accomplished, his work done, the people say, 'We did it ourselves'. This is likely to become increasingly important as businesses continue to replace financial or physical capital with knowledge capital. When the core competences of a business are largely in people's heads, then leading and managing those people becomes quite tricky. Bigger businesses are now looking carefully at how they can capture, share and retain that knowledge. Burston Marstellar, a large public relations company, for example, have recently appointed a chief knowledge officer.

When managers are asked to define leadership, they typically provide common sense answers such as:

- leadership involves getting others to do what you want;

- leaders motivate people to get things done;

- leaders provide a vision, a sense of meaning and purpose.

A leader for many people is someone who founds something new – a new movement, a new purpose, a new city. The word leader stems from the old English word 'laedere' which means to lead someone upon a journey – usually by going in front or by example. The idea of change is implicit in leadership as is the idea of example. Example holds a group together better than command. If people in a team see their leader operating or behaving in a particular way, they will tend to behave in that way. If a leader is seen as telling rather than doing the group will tend to want to ignore that person.

There is a difference, not always recognized, between leaders and managers, though the distinction is often confused when we talk about small business owner-managers. Perhaps we should talk about 'owner-leaders'. Leadership is about defining direction whereas management is about effective implementation to ensure the direction is followed. In total quality terms, leadership is about doing the right things, whilst management is about doing things right.

Leadership is about helping people. Leadership is not about leaders getting their own way but empowering people to do what they need to do. It is about ensuring that there are clear goals, about fitting the purpose of the organization to the environment, about assisting people to get the right things done, about setting high standards. Do not be afraid to lead. Set out clearly the direction or path you plan to take – and then follow it. Andy Grove argues that it doesn't even have to be the best direction, just strong and clear.

Leadership is a natural focus of the process within a group – the leader integrates the group and initiates structure. The leader is the person who comes up with ideas, who gives their group purpose and meaning. In some groups, the leader influences the group through force of personality which also makes possible feats of leadership of which ordinary men and women are incapable.

Exercise of influence over other people is considered to be a hallmark of leadership. Leaders change other people's behaviour through modelling desirable behaviours or communicating successfully the need for change.

Blake Mouton leadership grid

Jane Mouton and Robert Blake (1985) saw the two most important dimensions of leadership as being concern for production or task and concern for people. This implies a number of possible leadership styles, as illustrated in Figure 7.1.

The authoritarian manager (9,1) concentrates on the task but ignores the staff. The indulgent manager (1,9) looks after people

FIGURE 7.1   Leadership styles

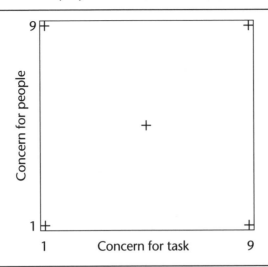

which may lead to a comfortable environment, but neglects the task. The minimal manager (1,1) has little concern for either people or task, exerting minimum effort. The compromise manager (5,5) compromises – a reasonable day's work without upsetting anyone. The integrative or team manager (9,9) develops commitment from people through promoting a source of common purpose and creates high production.

Where do you fit? What sort of leader, are you? There is an assumption in this that the best leadership style is a 9,9 style – high concern for people and high concern for task. As ever, there will be occasions when this is not necessarily the best style, but for much of the time such a style will hold you in good stead.

Action centred leadership

Another way of looking at leadership is John Adair's Action Centred Leadership. Adair suggests that leaders have to succeed in three interlinked activities: achieving the task, building the team and developing individuals. Developing staff will achieve the task. Building the team develops staff. Achieving the task is a requirement of the strategy. Adair offers a checklist for effective action centred leadership.

FIGURE 7.2 Action centred leadership

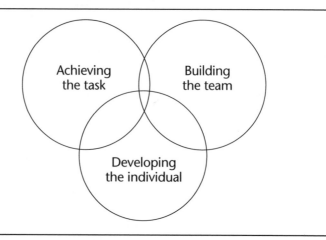

Task

- Be quite clear about the task. Communicate it with enthusiasm. Remind people of it often.

- Understand and demonstrate how the task fits into the strategic and operational objectives of the business.

- Plan how to accomplish it.

- Define and provide the resources needed, including the time and the authority required.

- Do everything possible to ensure that the management structure allows the task to be completed efficiently.

- Pace progress towards the achievement of the task.

- Evaluate results and compare them with original plans.

Team

- Set and maintain the team's objectives.

- Involve the team as a whole in the achievement of objectives.

- Maintain the unity of the team by coping effectively with conflict.

- Communicate regularly with the team face to face on matters of people, policy, progress and points for action.

- Consult with the team where possible before making decisions which affect them.

- Explain the business's results and achievements.

- Communicate changes in the business and how it will affect the team.

Individuals

Every leader must

- Provide a challenge and scope for development by:
  - setting and agreeing targets with everyone on an individual basis and reviewing them at regular intervals;
  - providing relevant training;
  - where appropriate using staff to train each other in relevant skills;
  - arranging or providing advice on any necessary external and internal contacts;
  - restructuring or grouping tasks to use people skills to the fullest;
  - rotating jobs to broaden experience;
  - providing scope for individuals to take greater responsibility;
  - training at least one deputy thoroughly.

- Make people feel valued by:
  - knowing their name and interests outside of work;
  - regularly monitoring and appreciating individual effort;
  - sharing an interest in what they hold important;
  - creating a good working environment by being approachable;
  - ensuring that everyone understands the importance of their contribution;
  - ensuring that everyone understands the function of the business.

- Recognize achievements by:
  - praising and communicating individuals' successes;
  - holding regular meetings with each individual to monitor and counsel;
  - providing guidance for a personal development programme ;
  - operating a fair and open policy linking salary to performance.

Organizational structure

In designing a suitable structure for your organization, there are a number of considerations to bear in mind, not least of which is how everyone will work towards achieving the strategy. Others include:

- number of staff required;

- basic design to undertake primary tasks (such as activities, marketing, accounting, personnel, etc.);

- preferred management culture;

- system of control.

Organizational structure offers security. The way in which you design and build an organization will depend on the individual and collective nature of the people who need to live in the organization as well as the environments in which the organization operates.

What sort of structure will suit the type of people who make up your business? Some people prefer a tight structure with well defined positions and procedures. Other people prefer a looser structure with less well defined roles and procedures.

How many tasks should a given position in the organization contain and how specialized should each task be? This will involve making decisions about who does what and telling people what they have to do.

To what extent can work be standardized for each position? This will involve decisions about rules and procedures and the degree to which the work is controlled by the worker or by the manager. What knowledge, skills and attitudes should be required for each position? On what basis should work positions be grouped into units and units into divisions?

How large should each unit be and how many individuals should report to a given manager? In formally structured organizations which are designed to ensure predictability, uniformity and reliability this can be an important question because of the amount of attention and time which managing people can take up in a loosely structured organization. Greater staff autonomy means that this is less important. Who makes the decisions? This question involves decisions about trust, delegation and the capacity for accurate decision making.

In the past, businesses have tended to adopt a hierarchical or role culture within departments, divisions or even subsidiary companies with very formal reporting mechanisms. They have also tended to divide their work functionally – into production, marketing, finance, etc. Increasingly, however, they are now breaking themselves up into smaller, autonomous businesses. Each business looks after its own production, its own marketing and its own finance. Increasingly, also, they are introducing teams, task cultures and matrix management.

Some businesses have introduced (not always totally successfully) a matrix management structure, where teams cut across functional boundaries, often where team leaders do not have line-management responsibility for members of their team particularly where people may be in more than one team simultaneously.

The advantages of a matrix structure are

- improves decision making where interests potentially conflict;

- involves more staff in decision making and so provides development opportunities;

- increases motivation of staff.

There are, of course, disadvantages also which include

- extends time required to reach decisions;

- lack of clarity of job and task responsibilities;

- lack of clarity about budget responsibilities;

- lack of clarity about priorities;

- potential for conflict.

To make a matrix structure work, managers must be prepared to collaborate widely and to be happy with at least a degree of ambiguity. Ideally one axis of the matrix should take the lead.

The organizational structure, and control mechanisms, that you choose will be dependent on your overall strategy and probably also on your position on the growth cycle described in chapter one. You will probably find yourself having quite a rigid, probably hierarchical structure at the outset. As the business grows, and as you grow in confidence, you will become happier to delegate. Indeed this is absolutely essential if the business is to grow. This still leaves a choice of organizational structure, but if you are serious about developing individual potential and encouraging individual entrepreneurship, then you will need a structure which allows these to flourish.

Teams

Groups in organizations can take many different forms – project teams, production teams, committees, quality circles, statistical process control teams, working groups, to name only a few. Whatever they are called they often frustrate and confuse their members. One of the oldest jokes about groups is that a camel is a horse designed by a committee.

Organizations large and small are full of people who hate working in groups because groups are often confused, frustrating and inefficient. They may also be threatening and stressful.

Yet groups have obvious advantages over individuals. They are more diverse, have greater knowledge and more time and energy. Groups can be a good way of improving communication. Nevertheless groups can over-respond to social pressures or individual domination, and personal goals can frustrate group purposes. As well as being productive, inducing commitment, developing people and creating excitement, groups can create stagnation, imprison people, induce conformity and leave people frustrated, feeling worthless and unproductive.

Building teams

According to Peter Drucker (1990), 'the more successful an organization becomes the more it needs to build teams.(Most) fumble and lose their way despite great ability at the top of a dedicated staff because they fail to build teams'.

The first thing that will indicate whether teams are appropriate is the nature of the work itself. Teams tend to perform better when they are involved in carrying out tasks which have clear short- or medium-term objectives.

The second indicator for team performance is the nature of the work environment and the management style which is accepted. A 'strong' management style where the team leader feels the need to tell people what to do or where the leader is very influential may not assist in team development. Leadership in a small group may have very different characteristics to the generally accepted model of what a leader or manager does. If you are reluctant to relinquish power, team building may be inappropriate.

In an organization which is structured by departments or where individuals concentrate on individual tasks with little relation between staff it may be inappropriate to consider team building.

The third indicator is the individuals who make up the team and the way in which they communicate. Teams do not need to be made up of similar individuals; indeed diversity will be an advantage in developing high performance teams and gives competitive advantage. Where the work requires little communication between staff, there is little reason to develop teams.

Team roles

There are a number of theories which suggest that people have specific roles which they will assume in most team activities. One of the most popular of these has been developed by Meredith Belbin (1981) who identified a number of team types.

- *Chairman* – Focuses on objectives; establishes the work roles and boundaries for other team members. Shows concern to use human resources effectively. Clarifies and sets objectives. Does not originate ideas. Summarizes and makes decisions when necessary – a good listener and communicator.

- *Shaper* – High nervous energy. Full of enthusiasm and drive. Continually looking for opportunities for action from ideas. Challenges and responds to challenges. Unites ideas and objectives. Seeks clarity and dislikes vagueness. Heavily involved in team's action and successes. The task leader of the group.

- *Plant* – The creative ideas person; tends to bring new insight and imagination to the group. Concerned with basics, not details. Tends to criticize. May withdraw if ideas are rejected.

- *Monitor evaluator* – Objective and serious. Concerned with idea analysis rather than idea generation. May lack motivation, but skilled in analysis and decision making. Solid and dependable.

- *Company worker* – The practical organizer. Concerned with order and feasibility. Methodical, efficient and systematic. Does not respond well to innovation or lack of structure. Pragmatically focused; may be inflexible, but responds to direction and adapts.

- *Resource investigator* – Friendly and sociable; enthusiastic and positive. The member who goes outside the team to explore and obtain new ideas and information. Enthusiasm may fade quickly; tends to be stimulated by others but is not an original thinker.

- *Team worker* – Sensitive, aware of feelings and emotions in the group. Tends to weld the team together. Builds on others' ideas. A popular and supportive member; uncompetitive and dislikes friction. A good listener and communicator.

- *Completer finisher* – Concerned with details and order, tends to worry over possible mistakes; communicates a permanent sense of urgency. May get bogged down in detail, losing sight of the main objective.

For Belbin, a balanced team needed to be made up of a full range of these roles. A missing role, or more than one person within the team occupying the same role, would weaken the team.

People who follow Belbin's approach attempt to manage relationships within teams by selecting compatible people, or people who occupy compatible roles. Whilst some research has shown this approach to be effective, roles can be unstable. They may change, depending on the nature of the task and the environment.

It is worth bearing these roles in mind however, when developing your team. You may be limited to the number and identity of people within your business but you can watch out for particular roles which are missing and to take steps to ensure those roles are, somehow, fulfilled.

High performance teams

The first Eagle team was a group of special force troops in the Second World War. This group outperformed any other commando group by reacting and destroying apparently unreachable targets with very light casualties.

Researchers assigned to the group found that one of the reasons for its success was its ability to change its structure to meet its circumstances or environment. For instance, in the planning stage everyone would chip in with suggestions and information. There were no leaders during the planning stages and all suggestions were treated equally.

This structure changed when the group went into action. The group adopted a formal, almost rigid structure with every member having a clearly assigned and agreed responsibility which had to be carried out with strict timing and precision.

This ability to change structure to fit the circumstances provided the best of both worlds. The participative structure in planning allowed all group members to contribute and thus increased the creativity of the group. The group in action took on a form where authority and roles had to be precise and communication was clearly defined.

The secret of Eagle team's success was the way in which it integrated all of the team frameworks into one in an informal 'culture' which underpinned enjoyment and creativity. The Eagle team became a team in the best sense of the word. We may want to surround ourselves with people who are 'just like us' but this will reduce the amount of creativity which we are likely to generate.

Developing teams can be very useful. Teams tend to get things done. Team building is not, however, a partial process. Done properly team building can release much of the energy locked within the organization. A partial process of team building may either not release the energy, in which case you've wasted your own time and effort, or release it in ways which you find hard to control.

Teams need to expend the energy which is generated by bringing them together. If you don't have anything for the team to work at, it will waste that energy on backbiting and politics or on completing the wrong task.

Generally when groups are free to choose their own leaders they tend to choose group members who will be able to maintain direction towards a goal, facilitate the achievements of tasks and ensure that the group stays together. Leaders may find that the short-term objective of measuring performance, may conflict with the longer term objectives of developing the group. Behaviours which foster the accomplishment of the task may be different to those which foster and develop the group. Some leaders are extremely effective in getting the job done whereas others are exceptionally skilled in the art of building satisfaction with and loyalty between members of the group.

Having a clear idea of task and structure will help in recruiting staff and then stimulating them to give of their best.

Recruitment

Hiring an employee is an expensive event. Be selective about who you hire. Where possible take time to get it right. Appointing the best of a poor set of applicants always returns to haunt you at a later date. Do not be afraid to go through the recruitment process more than once to find the right person. Make sure you feel as if they will fit in with the other staff. Staff dissatisfaction will result in a low quality service, an unpleasant atmosphere and a general disruption of the flow of business. You need therefore to take great care when recruiting and managing staff.

The Eagle Group recruited in a way which elicited commitment from its workers. They put up barriers to entry, demonstrating how hard it

FIGURE 7.3 Eligibility vs. suitability

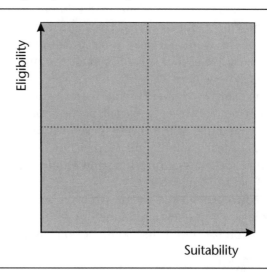

was to get into the group before they allowed the applicant in. This created a cohesiveness or sense of belonging to an elite group which engendered that elusive quality 'team spirit'. As noted earlier, recruit people who share your values and will behave in the way your culture demands.

Some of Belbin's early research looked at people's eligibility for a job (did they have the right qualifications, etc.) and their suitability for a job (would they fit the culture, could they work in teams, etc.).

You might expect to recruit people in the top right quadrant of Figure 7.3 – eminently eligible and eminently suitable. But if they are so eligible and suitable for your job, they may be for other jobs as well. So who do you go for? Many might go for those who are eligible and less suitable. My own organization goes for those who are suitable, but less eligible, aiming to develop people into the job. Not only does this ensure a better fit with the existing team, it also instils commitment and loyalty.

Delegation

You need to build the staff into a team who are all pulling in the same direction for the good of the organization. Each person must have a job that is directed towards fulfilling the objectives of the whole organization.

Delegation requires you to agree with all your staff a set of objectives. These need to be precise, challenging and achievable. If the targets are unrealistic then people will not even try; on the other hand, people need to be challenged if they are to achieve their full potential. These objectives then become the yardstick by which individual performance can be measured.

- Delegation is a contractual relationship which involves risk and exchange for both the delegator and the delegatee.

- Be clear about the task being delegated and deadlines and give guidelines if required.

- Ensure that the delegatee has understood.

- Check on progress (but not so often that it interferes with the person doing the work).

Remember that ineffective delegation will affect your workload, but effective delegation frees you to undertake more important tasks. Remember also that the human aspect is very important. The following pointers may help in reaching agreement for the business objectives.

- Individual responsibility and individual accountability is essential. Each department or activity must be the sole responsibility of just one person. This avoids buck-passing or confusion as to who is responsible. Moreover, that person must have the authority to exercise control. Responsibility and authority go hand in hand.

- If individuals are to work to a plan, they must feel committed to that plan. They will only be committed if they were consulted in the initial stages. If they had the opportunity to influence the original plan, then they will have a high degree of commitment to the outcome. The plan, of course, must fit the business's strategy and goals.

- Normally, each person is responsible for controlling some small part of the total. It can be a great help if every individual is aware of how their part interacts with the remainder, and why failure in one area (theirs) will affect others.

- Each person can only do so much. Their efforts should be focused where they will yield the greatest result.

- There is a very real danger of trying to exercise too much control over too many things. The principle of management by exception (that is, looking for variances from expectations and aiming to make corrections) is a sound one.

- All targets should be achievable.

- Ensure individuals are made aware of the results of their efforts. Praise regularly.

Staff appraisal

An important part of managing staff is appraisal, but for appraisal to be effective the organization needs goals and standards. Formal appraisal should assist in improving performance. It is not a way to punish poor performance. Appraisal should be continuous. If someone performs well, praise immediately. Similarly, poor performance should be discussed as quickly as possible. Formal appraisal should provide no surprises, for the appraiser or appraisee. The purpose of appraisal is to give you and your staff an opportunity:

- to review their overall performance during a given period of time;

- to ensure a shared understanding of the objectives of the job, and to demonstrate how those objectives fit into the business's strategy;

- to establish individual goals and aspirations – and training or development needs to achieve those;

- to evaluate current performance and to provide feedback of how you think they are performing;

- to establish an open and fair relationship based on trust;

- to provide you and your staff with a regular opportunity to agree an action plan or set of goals with an agreed timescale and, if necessary, to set targets to improve performance.

Appraisal is needed to encourage staff to become more effective in their work, giving an opportunity to summarize past performance and plan the future. The procedure must always be applied with common sense and flexibility. They should not be allowed to become a mechanical process or be seen as a substitute for informal day to day communication, coaching and constructive criticism. Through regular appraisal it should be possible to establish a rapport, thus improving morale and communications; agree strengths and weaknesses and as a means of raising efficiency and effectiveness; and, plan career development.

Performance and development

Developing your staff is an essential element in developing the organization, and giving it the skills, experience and competence to continue to grow. As you develop and train your staff you can relate the effectiveness of the training to staff performance. Development is about helping people improve their expertise and change their behaviour to meet changes in their work environment. Development might be undertaken by one to one training, peer training and group training or by less formal methods such as assignments, project work and effective delegation. In setting out to develop staff it is important to have clear objectives. Those objectives need to be linked to the organization's strategic objectives.

Clive Morton (1994) stresses the importance of investing in people. He suggests that businesses should:

- focus on the individual;

- provide continuous development, education and training with regular appraisal;

- involve everyone, for example, through quality circles or on advisory committees;

- communicate clearly and frequently with all the staff;

- emphasize the importance of developing teams;

- promote the importance of total quality management.

As soon as you start to employ people, you will have to consider how you are going to build them into a team, how the team is going to achieve the task and how you will develop each individual within the team.

The ability to encourage staff to increase their own motivational levels depends partly on enthusiasm and partly on policy. Policies and mechanisms for staff motivation are vital to success. Research has shown that in depth staff training leads to a greater commitment of the staff to the organization.

Whilst developing and motivating staff is crucial, do not overlook the importance of the board. Aim to recruit one or two non-executive directors who can make a real contribution to the business – through their knowledge, their experience and their network of contacts. Involve them in crucial decisions – especially in relation to strategic planning and financial forecasting. The executive directors work together every day, but the non-executives only come in periodically. So, you will have to engage in some board development and team building as well. All the directors, whether executive or non-executive, need to understand and trust each other.

Staff development – from vision ...

FIGURE 7.4

Not surprisingly, if training is going to be effective, it has to reinforce the business's goals and shorter term objectives, which have to help it progress towards achieving its strategic objectives.

Satisfactory completion of tasks, of course, requires that members of staff are assigned to those tasks, with specific personal objectives. Individual objectives and tasks should be discussed and agreed regularly.

... to development needs

There are, effectively, three ways in which a business identifies development needs.

First, they will arise from strategic decisions. My own organization, for example, decided some time ago to aim to provide incubator workspace – that is, workspace providing units for several businesses all within one building. Not only was this a major strategic decision requiring considerable investment, it also necessitated the training of existing staff and the appointment of staff who could bring specific skills immediately both to refurbish buildings as workspaces and to manage them subsequently. The introduction by the government of new rules to govern construction and design management required further training if we were to continue undertaking this area of our work.

If you are introducing total quality management and continuous improvement, you might train everyone who may answer a telephone to be able to deal with certain enquiries rather than just taking messages. You might have decided to become more reliant on technology for some of what you do – say, the Internet – which will require an appropriate training programme.

Second, development needs will arise from operational objectives and project tasks. A decision to offer NVQs as part of your management training programmes, for example, requires assessors and verifiers. You could buy in assessors and verifiers or you could choose to become an approved delivery centre, training your own staff to provide those functions.

The business's goals, strategic objectives, operational objectives and project tasks can then be summarized in a table, as shown in Table 7.1, together with the identified development requirements, though the requirements may be addressed in a number of ways – perhaps by buying in equipment, or by buying in a service, or by recruiting staff with appropriate skills, or by training existing members of staff.

There is a third way in which development needs arise. That is where members of staff or their line managers or team leaders identify weaknesses or development needs relating to the way those staff are carrying out current activities and where they are forecasting likely activities, say 6–18 months ahead, which may require training or personal development in advance.

It is important therefore, for all members of staff to set out and agree both short- and medium-term targets and objectives and to link a personal development plan to those objectives. Medium-term objectives will quickly become short-term objectives – but medium-term business objectives may require a short-term development plan if the business is to be able to achieve those objectives on time.

To capture everyone's personal development plan and to demonstrate a plan's relevance to the organization's objectives my own organization has included a specific section on its appraisal forms and introduced 'personal development records'.

On the appraisal form we record the objectives and tasks required of the individual by the company. These may imply elements of a personal development plan, in which case development or learning objectives and review dates are recorded.

TABLE 7.1 Organization development plan

Strategic objectives	Goals	Operational objectives	Project tasks	Development requirements
Develop new markets through joint ventures	Establish international joint venture	Identify suitable partner Prepare business plan and financial forecasts	Identify suitable products Identify appropriate markets Prepare detailed costings	Understand local legal requirements Learn foreign language
Improve means of storing and retrieving information throughout company through use of information technology	Establish intranet linking all staff and all offices	Install computer network Identify revised staffing needs Train staff	Install network Recruit additional staff Set up staff training programme Transfer existing systems Set up for use as intranet	Expertise in network administration Programming using HTML languages All staff to understand how to maximize benefit from system
Continuously improve effectiveness of staff	Achieve recognition as an Investor in People	Introduce continuing professional development	Revise appraisal system to reflect requirements of CPD Introduce personal development logs	Train line managers in appraisal skills

FIGURE 7.5

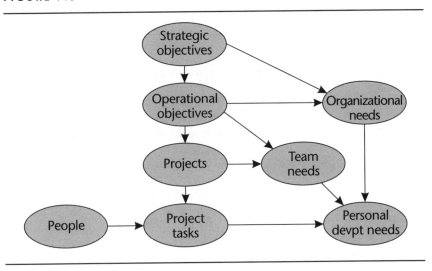

TABLE 7.2 Organizational and personal objectives

Organizational objectives	Personal development plan	
	Objectives	Review
Short term (0–6 months)		
Complete preparation of IT strategy	Be able to reconfigure computer network to use Windows NT	February
Install network	Be able to provide appropriate support to rest of staff	April
Set up staff training programme	Be able to manage additional staff	February
Transfer existing systems	Understand requirements of HTML and be able to use MS Front Page and MS Internet Explorer	January
Medium term (6-12 months)		
Set up network for use as intranet		

If this is done properly, it should ensure that each member of staff

- has clear work objectives and can see how these fit into the organization's strategy;

- can see how their job is likely to develop;

- understands what development work is required to help achieve their work objectives;

- undertakes training and personal development that is relevant to their job and avoids participating in programmes just for the sake of it.

It is then up to both you and your staff to ensure that they undertake their development plan.

All of these activities are recorded in a 'personal training record' which provides a permanent record for the member of staff – and, more importantly, a reminder which can act as the basis for a review of its effectiveness at the next appraisal.

Reviewing effectiveness ...

At the end of each training activity, staff should complete a simple evaluation form intended to assist in assessing the immediate value of specific training inputs.

FIGURE 7.6

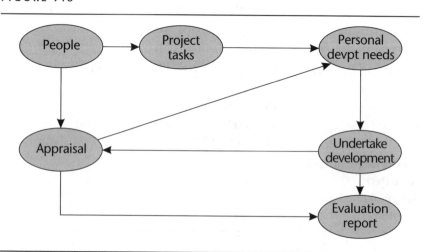

At the person's next appraisal, there can be a review of progress made towards achieving their development objectives. Has the person put into effect what they have learned? Has their behaviour changed? The appraisal interview also provides an opportunity to review individual tasks and development objectives and to review and update the personal development plan.

... and economy

You will also be concerned about the cost of training and whether the business is getting value for money. Ideally, you will want to determine whether the cost of the training (in fees and staff time) is more than covered by the benefits (in improved effectiveness, productivity, efficiency, etc.). Where the development is the acquisition of a practical skill it is relatively easy to measure benefits and effectiveness. For development needs which are more subjective evaluation may depend on a combination of factors which include assessment by the individual and the stakeholders in that individual development. The stakeholders include the appraiser/line manager, external customers of the project or task, etc.

Don't be reluctant to admit that you, too, need to learn as the business grows. It can be too easy to ignore your own shortcomings when you're surrounded by people who defer to you simply because you're the boss. Engage periodically in rigorous self-assessment.

It may help you, both in discussing and agreeing individual development plans and in mentoring staff as they progress through their objectives if you have some understanding of the different ways in which people learn.

Understanding the learning process

People develop their skills in different ways – on the job training, informal reading, more formal distance learning, participation in formal training programmes, etc. There are four main ways in which people learn:

- *Intuitive*: the underlying, natural process which takes place all the time often without you even being conscious that it is happening.

- *Incidental*: learning which is triggered by events which prompt you to think about what happened and why. This sort of learning is more conscious.

- *Retrospective*: a more systematic approach in which you think more rigorously about activities and events and analyse what you have learned from them.

- *Prospective*: this is the most active type of learning in which you plan carefully what you hope to learn from a particular experience and then review carefully afterwards.

Considerable research has been undertaken by David Kolb (1974), who identified four stages in the learning process (Figure 7.7). The first stage is to plan what you want to learn and how you intend to do it. Is one of the types of learning outlined above more suited than another to your need? The second stage is to take action, that is, to undertake the training. The third stage is to reflect on what you have learned from the experience. This may take some time and will continue as you try to put into effect what you have learned. The last stage is to put this into the context of your work, concluding whether what you have learned is relevant or valid and deciding how you will put that learning to practical use. That takes you back to the beginning when you can start to think about what further learning may be required.

Learning styles

It will be no surprise to you that people learn in different ways. And most people find that they learn better if they adopt an approach with which

FIGURE 7.7

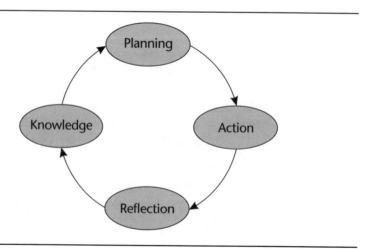

they are comfortable. Extensive research, particularly by Peter Honey and Alan Mumford (1982) suggests that there are four learning styles:

- *Activists*: people who learn best from relatively short, perhaps intensive, immediate and active involvement in practical tasks. Activists are always ready to complete the first two stages of the learning cycle but are more reluctant to complete the last two. Activists tend to favour intuitive and incidental types of learning.

- *Reflectors*: people who learn best from situations and activities in which they can stand back, listen and observe before they act. They are consequently most effective in the review component of the learning cycle. Reflectors tend to favour the retrospective type of learning.

- *Theorists*: people who prefer to place their learning in the context of a theory or model. They perform best in the conclusion, or knowledge, stage of the learning cycle. Theorists tend to favour retrospective and prospective types of learning.

- *Pragmatists*: people who learn best when they see a clear practical link between the subject matter and a personal or work based problem or opportunity. Pragmatists are particularly effective in the planning stage of the learning cycle. Pragmatists tend to favour the prospective type of learning – provided it is directed towards a practical goal.

You may want to encourage people with whom you are working to think about the learning style that suits them best. You can then aim to match the way that personal development is delivered to match their preferred learning style.

Learning companies

Encouraging personal development will undoubtedly help individual members of staff. But companies have to become institutional learners as well.

You need to encourage everyone to learn – and somehow you need to capture that learning institutionally. Corporate learning is difficult to achieve but it is essential for business success that learning, often as simple as just listening to customers, can drive the business's competitiveness and drive its quest for innovation. A formal approach to personal development will assist in ensuring effective institutional learning. It has been suggested (Garvin, 1993) that learning organizations are good at five key activities:

- systematic problem solving;

- experimentation with new approaches;

- learning from their own experience;

- learning from the experience and practice of others;

- transferring new knowledge quickly and efficiently throughout the organization.

How does your business measure up against these criteria?

Companies that do aim to learn often look for other knowledge hungry companies – to share ideas, to network and to learn still more. They also seem to share a desire for having a high process for promoting a learning culture. Unipart has its own 'university', the Unipart U, Anglian Water has set up its 'University of Water' and McDonald's has its Hamburger University.

Smaller businesses do not have the resources to be quite such high profile learning organizations, but you can, nevertheless, promote a culture of learning and sharing.

Peter Senge (1990) suggests that it is important to encourage and engage in personal development. He argues that building a shared vision is important: if the leaders of an organization share a vision, reinforced by a common purpose and by shared values and behaviour, then 'people excel and learn'.

Working with people, and developing people, is crucial to the modern business. This is likely to become more important as businesses increasingly become knowledge based businesses. As de Geus observes (1997), 'managers have had to shift priorities from running companies to optimise capital to running companies to optimise people. In these companies, people are the carriers of knowledge and therefore the source of competitive advantage.' He goes on to suggest, perhaps a little simplistically, that strategy is a development of a business's ability to learn though the message is clear: 'the organisation's ability to learn faster (and possibly better) than the competition becomes its most sustainable competitive advantage'. Or as Eric Hoffer (1997) says: 'In times of drastic change, it is the learners who inherit the future. The learned usually find themselves equipped to live in a world that no longer exists.'

In other words, everyone who works in the business has to be sensitive to the environment and the market place, has to draw conclusions and share those conclusions with the rest of the business. Part of your role as a leader is to stimulate and encourage that sensitivity and that sharing and learning – and feed it back into the strategic thinking cycle.

Conclusion

As the market place changes and the environment changes, businesses, too, have to change. Change is never easy – people are always too comfortable with the *status quo*. Strategic thinking is intended to move the business forward, reacting to those external influences, whereas the business will have a sructure, and possibly a culture, rooted in history. If you want the business to progress, you have to be clear about the changes that are necessary and you have to lead. At the same time, the business has to learn and adapt. It has been suggested that 80 per cent of all organizational transformations fail, apparently because they do not support their people through the transformation; it could be, however, that change is not supported because of a poor understanding of why it is necessary.

Managing change can be one of the hardest requirements of any manager. Change can be incremental – slow, perhaps almost unnoticed – or it can be sudden – perhaps caused by unexpected changes in the external environment. Change in your business, however, needs to be managed.

As with so many other aspects of management the Plan-Do-Check-Act cycle is a helpful model. The first step is to understand the process that is to be changed and to identify whether, indeed, there is a need for change. This may require consideration of where you are now, where you want to be, and how you think you are going to get there. The big picture provides the strategic direction. The changes, particularly incremental changes, provide the short-term operational requirements. Having identified the options, it is possible to take decisions on the appropriate changes, to seek commitment from all the staff involved, to plan the change and then to implement it. People are usually unhappy with change and resist it, preferring to stick with the *status quo*, so there is a need first to 'unfreeze'.

Take time to communicate the reasons for change, the objectives desired from the changes and the benefits expected. You need at the very least to win acquiescence from your staff and other key stakeholders. Ideally, you want to win enthusiasm – generated by a desire to help the business grow and an expectation of being able to share in the benefits. If people have been properly trained and developed, then it is highly likely that they will be supportive of change.

In summary, your staff will be more willing to accept change if they:

- understand why change is necessary;

- know what needs to be changed;

- know specifically what changes need to take place;

- understand how the change will happen;

- are able to contribute to the change;

- understand the perceived benefits of the change;

- understand how the success of the change will be measured.

The changes can then be implemented. It is usually necessary then to 'freeze' the new position to prevent people slipping back into their old ways. Once the changes have been implemented, the effects of the change can be reviewed and, if necessary, further action or further change can be implemented.

If you have, or can develop, a culture which is comfortable with change, even if not wildly enthusiastic, then this will undoubtedly help.

Your staff are the essential component in helping you to achieve your goals. You will need to work hard to ensure that they share your goals and to lead and motivate them towards achieving those goals. Having clear objectives for training and development will help not only in motivating staff but also in equipping them with the skills required for the business to change and grow effectively. Being comfortable with change yourself will help you to manage the change required for the business's development.

CHAPTER EIGHT

Strategy checklist to help your business grow

Keep it simple

It's all too easy to get carried away preparing detailed strategic plans and allowing the thinking and the planning to become an end in itself rather than a mechanism for guiding you to success and prosperity. Do take time to think and to plan periodically – preferably with your colleagues, preferably away from the office to avoid distractions and, possibly, with one or two third parties such as a consultant or accountant or even a couple of customers if you know them well enough.

Every software package now comes with a detailed book about its use – and an aide memoir summarizing the key commands. Let me, then, try to sum up the key messages from this book into a short checklist that you may find helpful as you are developing your own strategic framework.

Look out

Scan the horizon – what is happening in your market place? What do customers want now? What might they want in the future? How is the market place changing? What are your competitors doing? What are their strengths and weaknesses?

What is happening in the wider environment? Undertake a PEST analysis. What are the opportunities and threats posed both by the market place and by that wider environment.

Compare your own business practices with the best. Benchmark yourself in an effort to improve what you do. But always remember that benchmarking will not help you to surpass the best. For that, you need to innovate.

Look ahead

Be foresightful. Construct scenarios. Ask yourself 'what if ...' questions. Add to your analysis of opportunities and threats. Anticipate the needs of your customers.

What will your next product or service be? And the one after that?

Look in

Study your own business. Do the key staff have similar values? What drives you? What does the company believe in? Can you define the culture – the way we do things round here – particularly, the management culture?

Are the company's values consistent with its purpose and goals? Are the values likely to lead to problems with potential customers? Would the community be happy with your values?

Does the culture support what the business is trying to do? Does it encourage initiative and responsibility (if that is necessary)? Does it encourage change – or resist it?

What resources – human, financial, facilities – are available? What additional resources can you attract?

Where have you come from? What have been the defining moments in the development of your business to date? What are the strengths and weaknesses of your business? What are your core competences? What is it that gives you your competitive edge?

Ensure that you have in place appropriate management information and financial systems, to give rapid access to information, but do not over-complicate.

Define a direction

Be purposeful – define, carefully, your business's purpose. What do you do? Are you focusing on your core competences? Who are your key customers? What is your generic strategy – differentiation or cost leadership?

Where are you going? Do you have a vision of where you want to be in, say, five years' time? Do you have some big hairy audacious goals that you and your staff can rally behind? Are your purpose and goals consistent with and supported by your values?

How are you aiming to position yourself in the market?

Does all of your business share your vision?

FIGURE 8.1   Hierarchy of objectives

Organizational purpose
(what we do)

Values
(what we believe in)

Culture
(how we do things)

Vision
(where we are going)

Strategic objectives
(a five year view)

Operational objectives
(a one to two year view)

Performance indicators
(targets and milestones)

Define objectives

Do you have clear strategic objectives, operational objectives and performance measures in the areas of

- business activities?

- finance?

- marketing?

- quality?

- staff development?

Do the purpose, goals, objectives and performance measures hang together coherently? Do you focus on customers' needs?

Adopt a total quality approach. Aim for continuous improvement.

Do you have a sufficiently small number of targets to make monitoring relatively straightforward? Are the targets demanding but realistic? Do you monitor regularly? When you do identify variances, do you take appropriate corrective action?

Organize for success

Have you thought about your role as a leader? Do you lead – guide, inspire, motivate – or do you spend too much time 'managing'? Do you recognize, and reward, success?

Do you aim for all your staff to achieve their potential? Do you provide challenges which stretch?

Does your management structure reflect the strategy that you have adopted? Does it provide effective monitoring and control mechanisms? Does it give staff the opportunity to develop, or surpass, their potential? Does it encourage communication?

Are individuals given the appropriate responsibility and authority? Empower staff. Are they held accountable for their performance and that of their teams? Encourage a team approach.

Do you have in place appropriate staff development mechanisms? Do you encourage staff to engage in training, education and personal development?

How do you encourage, capture and share institutional learning?

Above all, remember that thinking strategically is not something that you do once – and then forget about. It is something that should happen on an almost continuous basis. Every time you make a decision for the business, it may have a strategic implication for the business.

It can be very easy, once a business is up and running and doing moderately well, to become too comfortable and too insulated from the wider world. You will need to be pro-active, therefore, in looking out, looking ahead and looking in. Put in place mechanisms to help you – read *The Economist* and relevant trade journals and network widely.

Most importantly, however, take time out from your business periodically to review and, if necessary, to update your strategy. That way you can ensure the strategy is right for your business – and thus maximize your chances for growth, success and prosperity.

References

Adair, John (1983) *Action Centred Leadership*, Talbot Adair.

Ansoff, H.I. (1987) *Corporate Strategy*, Penguin.

Bartlett, Christopher and Ghoshal, Sumantra (1994) 'Changing the role of top management: beyond strategy to purpose', *Harvard Business Review*, November–December.

Bartlett, Christopher and Ghoshal, Sumantra (1995) 'Changing the role of top management: beyond systems to people', *Harvard Business Review*, May–June.

Belbin, Meredith (1981) *Management Teams – Why They Succeed or Fail*, Heinemann.

Blake, R. and Mouton, J. (1985) *Managerial Grid III*, Gulf.

Burton Group plc (1993) *Annual Report*.

Campbell, Andrew, Devine, Marion and Young, David (1990) *Sense of Mission*, Economist Books Ltd.

The Economist (1997) Reporting on Bill Gross, 8 March.

Collins, John and Porras,Gerry (1994) *Built to Last: Successful Habits of Visionary Companies*, Harper Collins.

Department of Trade and Industry(DTI)/Confederation of British Industry(CBI) (1994) 'Competitiveness – how the best UK companies are winning', HMSO.

Doerr, John, (1997) *New Yorker*, 11 August.

Drucker, Peter (1968) *The Practice of Management*, Pan Books (originally published 1955 Wm. Heinemann Ltd.).

Drucker, Peter (1974) *Management: Tasks, Responsibilities, Practices*, Butterworth-Heinemann.

Drucker, Peter (1990) *Managing the Non-profit Organisation*, Butterworth-Heinemann.

The Economist (1997) 2 August.

Garratt, Bob (1996) *The Fish Rots from the Head*, Harper Collins.

Garvin, David (1993) 'Building a learning organisation', *Harvard Business Review*, July–August.

Gates, Bill (1994) *Wired*.

Geus, Arie de (1988) 'Planning as learning', *Harvard Business Review*, March–April.

Geus, Arie de (1997) *The Living Company*, Nicholas Brealey.

Ghoshal, Sumantra (1996) *Management Today*, December.

Greiner, Larry (1972) 'Evolution and revolution as organisations grow', *Harvard Business Review*, July–August.

Grove, Andy (1997) *Only the Paranoid Survive*, Harper Collins Business.

Hamel, Gary (1997) *The Economist*, 1 March.

Hamel, Gary (1997) *Management Today*, July.

Hamel, Gary and Prahalad, C.K. (1994) *Competing for the Future*, Harvard Business School Press.

Handy, Charles (1985) *The Gods of Management*, Pan.

Herkströter, Cor (1996) *Co-operating to Create our Future: A Personal View of the Way Ahead for Europe*, Shell.

Hoffer, Eric (1997) quoted in the annual report of the Strategic Planning Society.

Honey, P. and Mumford, A.C. (1982) 'Learning styles and learning skills', *Journal of Management and Development*, Vol.1, No.2.

Johnson, Gerry and Scholes, Kevan (1993) *Exploring Corporate Strategy*, third edition, Prentice Hall.

Kaplan, Robert and Norton, David (1992) 'The balanced scorecard – measures that drive performance', *Harvard Business Review*, January–February.

Kolb, D.A., Rubin, I.M. and McIntyre, J.M. (1974) *Organisational Psychology – an Experiential Approach*, Prentice Hall.

Maslow, Abraham (1954) *Motivation and Personality*, Harper & Row.

Mintzberg, Henry (1994) *The Rise & Fall of Strategic Planning*, Prentice Hall.

Moody-Stuart, Mark (1997) 'It's more than just business', speech presented at the Global Forum Conference, Konya, Turkey, 6 October.

Morton, Clive (1994) *Becoming World Class*, Macmillan.

Moss-Kanter, Rosabeth, (1997) *World Class: Thriving Locally in the Global Economy*, Touchstone Books.

Onians, Richard (1995) 'Making small fortunes: success factors in starting a business', *RSA Journal*, May.

Peters, Glen (1996) *Beyond the Next Wave*, Pitman Publishing.

Peters, Tom (1982) *In Search of Excellence*, Harper & Row.

Peters, Tom (1987) *Thriving on Chaos*, Alfred P Knopf.

Porter, Michael (1980) *Competitive Strategy*, Free Press.

Porter, Michael (1985) *Competitive Advantage*, Free Press.

Royal Society for the encouragement of Arts, Manufactures and Commerce (RSA), (1995) 'Tomorrow's company: the role of business in a changing world', *RSA Journal*, January.

Schwartz, Peter (1997) *The Art of the Long View*, John Wiley.

Senge, Peter (1990) *The Fifth Discipline*, Century Business.

Stern Stewart (undated) *An EVA Financial Management System*, Stern Stewart, 40 West 57th Street, New York, NY 10019, USA.

Sunday Times (1995) 10 December.

Sunday Times (1997) Quoting Eddie Jordan, 13 July.

Sunter, Clem (1992) *The New Century: Quest for the High Road*, Human & Rousseau and Tafelberg.

Tzu, Lao (1989) *Tao Te Ching*, in Adair, John *Great Leaders*, Talbot Adair Press.

Vonderembse, Mark A. and White, Gregory P. (1996) *Operations Management, Methods and Strategies*, third edition, West Publishing Company.

Walsh, Ciaren (1993) *Key Management Ratios*, FT/Pitman Publishing.

Waterman, Robert (1994) *The Frontiers of Excellence*, Nicholas Brealey Publishing.

Wybrew, John (1992) 'Trends affecting small businesses and their implications', in *Changing Patterns of Employment*, Livewire.

Index

4Ps 96, 114

acquisition 112
Action centred leadership 139
Adair, John 139
Agromasina 85
appraisal 150
attractiveness 99

Balanced Scorecard 108
Baring Venture Partners 16
Barnevik, Percy 134
Bartlett, Christopher 71, 116
behaviour 67, 85
Belbin, Meredith 145
beliefs 68
Ben & Jerry's 92
benchmarking 39, 90, 109
benefits 84, 97, 113
Blake, Robert 138
brands 95
British Biotech 89
British Telecom 69
Burton Group 22, 87, 125

Campbell, Andrew 85
capital employed 117
capital investment 125
cause and effect 43
change management 161
chess 65
club culture 11
Collins, John 68, 75, 89
competitive advantage 84

competitive position 99
competitor analysis 24
continuous improvement 126
Co-operative Bank 71
core competence 87
cost leadership 82, 92
critical success factors 110
culture 75
customer profiling 22

Daimler Benz 125
de Geus, Arie 45, 52, 67, 160
delegation 148
Delphi analysis 50
Deming, W. Edwards 13
development, staff 152, 160
differentiation 21, 82, 92, 115
direction 138
distribution 114
diversification 102
Drucker, Peter 6, 10, 81, 84, 107, 144

economic forces 31
Economic Value Added 123
effectiveness, training 156
efficiency 124
environmental forces 34
ethics 68
European Foundation for Quality
   Management 41
European Union 36
EVA 123

features 97, 113

financial objectives 115
five forces model 19
focus 86
football manager 2
foresight 4, 9, 49
Foresight Research Centre 59

gardening 1
Garratt, Bob 8, 16
Garvin, David 39
Gates, Bill 30
gearing 120
General Electric business screen 99
General Motors 32
generic strategies 91
Ghoshal, Sumantra 71, 89, 116
goals 2, 3, 7, 89, 103
Greiner, Larry 11
Grove, Andy 9, 138
growth 11, 100

Hamel, Gary 10, 24, 90, 95
Handy, Charles 78
Hierarchy of Needs 97
Hoffer, Eric 160
Honey, Peter 159
hurdle rate 125
Hydro Technologies 90, 102

impact analysis 51
industry attractiveness 99
information management 44
innovation 84, 88
Intel 20, 29, 95
internal rate of return 126
ISO9000 127

job analysis 81
John Lewis Partnership 77
Johnson, Gerry 10, 82
joint venture 112

Kaizen 15
Kaplan, Robert 108
Kolb, David 158

Lao Tzu 137
leadership 137, 144
learning 157

learning companies 13, 159
leverage 122
Levi Strauss 71, 86
liquidity ratios 122

management styles 78
market segmentation 22, 94
marketing mix 96, 114
marketing objectives 112
Maslow, Abraham 97
MEASURE 106
Mintzberg, Henry 9, 15
mission statement 86
Morton, Clive 151
Moss-Kanter, Rosabeth 37
motivation 135
Mouton, Jane 138
Mumford, Alan 159

net present value 126
networking 36
niche marketing 22, 93
Nissan 32, 70
non-executive directors 151
Norton, David 108

objectives 105
Octo Industrial Design 75, 86
Onians, Richard 5, 45
operational plan 2
opportunities 2, 45

partnership sourcing 131
payback 126
people 135
performance measures 105
performance, staff 151
personal training record 156
PEST analysis 26
Peters, Tom 18, 39
place 114
Plan-Do-Check-Act 77, 111, 161
planning 4, 15
political forces 35
Porras, Gerry 68, 75, 89
Porter, Michael 10, 19, 91
positioning 92, 94
Prahalad, C.K. 10, 24, 907 95
product 97

productivity 124
profitability 116
Project North East 69
promotion 114
purchasing 131
purpose 2, 5, 9, 85, 105

quality objectives 126

ratio tree 119
ratios 106, 115
recruitment 147
resources 44, 81, 125
return on capital employed 117, 126
role culture 12, 142

sales pyramid 113
satisfaction 114
scenario planning 53, 60
scenarios 50, 52
Scholes, Kieran 10, 82
Schwartz, Peter 54
Senge, Peter 160
sensitivity 80
Shell 53, 58, 73
social forces 26
Solution Design Consultants 86
staff 134
stakeholders 7
strategy 8, 85, 91, 105
strengths 1, 66

structure 142
style 67
supply chains 131

targets 105, 141
task culture 13, 143
team roles 145
teams 3, 144
technological forces 28
threats 2, 3, 45
tolerance 80
Tomorrow's Company 5
total quality management (TQM) 126

University of Northumbria 39

Valley Trust 87
value, added 84, 123
values 5, 24, 67, 85
virtual reality 31
vision 9, 89

Waterman, Robert 134
weaknesses 2, 3
Welch, Jack 107
world class 4

Xerox 42
Xtralite 103

Yeoman Pressings 136